A GUIDE TO PRAYER

IN TODAY'S ENGLISH AND WITH A STUDY GUIDE

ISAAC WATTS

GODLIPRESS TEAM

© Copyright 2022 by GodliPress. All rights reserved.

This book is copyright protected. You cannot amend, distribute, sell, use, quote or paraphrase any part, or the content within this book, without the consent of the author or publisher, except in the case of brief quotations embodied in critical articles or reviews.

Scripture quotations are from The ESV® Bible (The Holy Bible, English Standard Version®), copyright © 2001 by Crossway, a publishing ministry of Good News Publishers. Used by permission. All rights reserved

CONTENTS

Introduction	v
Preface	ix
1. WHAT IS PRAYER?	1
Calling on God	1
Praise	2
Confession	5
Requests	7
Pleading	11
Declaration	17
Thanksgiving	20
Blessing	23
Amen	23
Study Guide	24
2. THE GIFT OF PRAYER	27
What Is the Gift of Prayer?	28
Types of Prayer	29
The Content of Prayer	42
The Method of Prayer	54
Expression in Prayer	59
The Voice in Prayer	75
Gestures in Prayer	81
Family Prayer	87
General Suggestions on the Gift of Prayer	89
Study Guide	94
3. THE GRACE OF PRAYER	97
The Difference Between the Grace and the Gift	97
Grace in Prayer	100
Grace in the Parts of Prayer	103
Suggestions to Gain the Grace of Prayer	107
Study Guide	111

4. THE SPIRIT OF PRAYER	112
Proof of the Spirit's Help in Prayer	113
How the Spirit Helps in Prayer	122
Cautions on the Spirit's Help	134
Suggestions to Keep the Spirit of Prayer	145
Study Guide	155
5. REASONS FOR LEARNING TO PRAY	157
Prayer Is Corresponding With Heaven.	159
Prayer Is Necessary and Useful for Christians.	162
Praying Is a Joy and Advantage for Our Hearts	164
Prayer Honors God and Christians.	166
Prayer Is Simple With the Holy Spirit's Help	170
There Are Consequences for Not Praying	175
Study Guide	177
About Isaac Watts	181
Bibliography	185

INTRODUCTION

As we are aware, there are many books on prayer. Probably too many to choose from. Most of them are more well-known than the one written and produced by Watts several hundred years ago. So, what makes this guide different? How is it more useful? Is it even essential?

Isaac Watts, himself, admits that there is no need to write another book on the same subject; regurgitating facts, knowledge, and ideas that have been covered already. In his preface, he even encourages readers to find those other publications in order to gain more insight into facets of prayer that he does not cover.

So why do we need to read Watts' *A Guide to Prayer*?

The answer can be found in the approach Isaac Watts brings to prayer—specifically, his unique gifts and talents as an educated theologian and philosopher.

Almost every Christian has heard the hymns, *When I Survey the Wondrous Cross*, *Joy to the World*, and *Our God, Our Help in Ages Past*. Watts' fame as a songwriter precedes him in this area. The beauty of his words and the reverence in his tunes are still enough to move us into God's presence to this day.

They almost overshadow the fact that in his day he was an extremely gifted writer and thinker. His skills in forming, laying out, and executing arguments set his works apart. His book on logic—a detailed insight and guide into what it is, how to use it, and the products of rational thinking—became the standard textbook for every university during his lifetime.

In using a similar technique to tackle the subject of prayer, this volume stands out from others covering the same topic. Instead of a soaring, beautifully-penned composition, Watts uses lists, rules, and practical examples. It is his basis for the whole book—signposts and specific guidelines to understand prayer, how to attain it, and how to use it.

This approach becomes very clear in the first chapter under the different parts of prayer, as Watts makes the effort to list samples of actual words that you can use in your own devotions. This detailed assistance is fantastic for those of us who understand the concept but are at a loss to put it into action.

Although Watts makes it clear throughout the book that there is room for us to express our hearts and be led by the Holy Spirit, he is a firm believer in order. He gives us examples of chaotic, confused prayers and how they dishonor God. To help us in this regard, there are rules to follow if we are to succeed in becoming Christians that pray according to the way God ordained it and the way the Spirit often works. Not only that, but he couples these with further suggestions on how to accomplish these regulations.

It may sound legalistic, but Watts' reason and heart for doing so are very clear—this is a manual, a teaching tool, a guide. Many of us see others praying with such passion and eloquence, but we are too afraid to ask how to get to that same place. Or perhaps, we struggle with characteristics that trip us up when we want to learn. This book provides detailed answers to every problem or question.

True to his style of thinking, Watts even takes the time to list the objections and arguments we might have to some of his statements—and he provides suitable, biblical replies to keep us focused on the goal of becoming people that pray correctly and effectively.

To be able to access such a treasure of knowledge and direction in our own modern English is an incredible blessing. Written almost 300 years ago, we have done our best to hold on to the heart and ideas without losing anything along the way, and bring this classic in understandable, readable sentences and phrases.

Not only that, but as an added tool, you will find a study guide with brief summaries, tips on how to enhance your time of reflection, and questions that will lead you into a deeper understanding of not only the chapters, but yourself in connection to prayer.

To ask if we need another book on prayer is to miss the point. To see what Isaac Watts brings to a topic many of us struggle to get a grip on is where this wonderful guide shines. It should be on our shelves alongside the other great classics that encourage and equip us as Christians.

Finding God, entering his presence, talking with him, knowing his heart as he knows our hearts; this is the goal of prayer—that God may be all to us as we become all for him.

> "Love so amazing, so divine, demands my soul, my life, my all"

PREFACE

Prayer is such a large and necessary part of Christianity that any assistance is always welcome to those wanting to learn. The inner and spiritual performance of prayer is taught in many excellent books and sermons, but the regular habit has been neglected. The form, method, and expression, as well as voice and gesture, are hardly ever explained, so most Christians have no clear knowledge about them. Yet when these aspects are performed correctly and spiritually, they have a powerful influence on the soul. Both nature and the Bible give us various instructions about different methods of prayer. Now, while there are many institutes of learning that teach us to reason logically and to speak well among people, why should there be hardly any teaching about the rules of speaking to God?

It is wonderful that there are so many ministers using the gift of prayer and doing so honorably and effectively every day, yet they are content to point others to it simply by following guidelines. So, we are taught to pray, as some claim to teach French and Latin—only by rote and repetition. But those who learn by rule as well as by imitation are far better prepared to speak those languages properly on every occasion.

I am convinced that one reason for this neglect has been the divisions among us. Most normal, upstanding people have been discouraged from even trying to master prayer, while the fanatics are divided into two extremes. Some argue for pre-composed, set formats of prayer and will not worship God in any other way. They do not need any other instructions except to be taught to read well, since the words, content, and method of their prayers are already fixed. Other passionate people, in extreme opposition to them, indulge in the freedom of thought and expression, so they will not limit the Spirit and return to carnal rituals because of confinement to rules.

But if the leaders of one side of the debate spent as much time learning to pray as they do reading liturgies and justifying their opinions; and if those on the other side, together with their cautions against quenching the Spirit, had practiced this divine skill themselves, and taught Christians how to pray; I believe the habit of free prayer would be more accepted, and the fire of this controversy would never have brought as much destruction as it already has.

Reasons and Inspiration

My idea was to write a prayer book without techniques and rules, and I have tried to stick to the middle between the mistakes of those competing Christians on either side.

In describing the nature of prayer, I have not expanded much on each aspect, but I have been careful to divide it into all its necessary parts, so that younger Christians might have some proper content and method when addressing God.

The gift, grace, and spirit of prayer have become a subject of ridicule. Some have completely given it up and instead, mock and criticize it. Others have only encouraged this thinking by making it sound like some ultra-spiritual, holy thing. So, I have tried to keep the terms clear and rational and explain them as a wise teacher who is not swayed by opinions and factions. My thinking is that normal Christians might easily understand what is meant by the gift of praying and praying by the Spirit; and that they might not expose themselves to the criticism of talking without meaning or be accused of fanaticism.

Talking about the gift or ability to pray, I speak generally and specifically—how to achieve it and the mistakes people often make. I believe we learn to avoid errors much better by a clear picture of the mistakes than by a list of rules and suggestions.

This will put me in a difficult position with some readers. If I describe the wrong way of speaking and acting using a general tone, I will be criticized because my examples are taken from real life; while others will suspect that those examples are only of weaker Christians. On the other hand, if I present the worst-case scenarios, my opponents would not believe that preachers could be guilty of them; while others would say I was irrelevant for exposing faults that nobody practices.

I would rather choose the lesser of two evils—it is better to be irrelevant than to advertise foolishness. Therefore, I have detailed those mistakes in the extreme, that they might never be practiced by anyone. To do this, I have borrowed examples of improper expressions from older writers; and several of the descriptions of incorrect ways of speaking and movement from obscure public speakers. I was obliged to do this because the prayers I have heard and observed did not line up.

If I had described some average mistakes, weaker people may have tried to defend them, not understanding why they are wrong. But now the examples I have given are so inappropriate and ridiculous that everyone will be convinced that they should be avoided, and younger Christians when they learn to pray will keep away from these types of prayer. But it is not easy to bring change without offending someone.

So that this book is not incomplete, I have added a short chapter about the grace of prayer, even though there is much written and preached about it.

In speaking about the Spirit of prayer, I have tried to remove all controversies by giving the most natural explanations of verses that refer to this matter; and by adding a reasonable and clear account of the Spirit's role in assisting people in prayer.

At the end of these chapters, I have added many rules, taken from logic, observations, and the Bible, as to how every Christian can achieve these blessings. The book's conclusion has a sincere appeal to desire the best gifts and to seek after the most excellent way of performing prayer.

Perhaps some people may wonder why I do not recommend the Lord's prayer as a perfect pattern for all Christians. But it is my opinion that divine wisdom gave it for other purposes. Later, I may write about the Lord's prayer, together with a short essay or two I wrote on the personal ministry of Jesus on earth.

These were first written for a group of young men who wanted to learn to pray, and this might excuse the style. It has sat silent for several years and has resisted many requests to be published, in the hope that it be refined a bit more. But only God knows when I shall have health and time to put my thoughts on paper. I am convinced that it is better for me to do something for God, even if it is imperfect, than to be guilty of delaying it to please myself.

I have been careful to avoid controversy and express myself to not be offensive to any clear-thinking Christians. Yet if I have said anything that will upset my younger readers, I must ask them not to throw the whole book away and deprive themselves of what they might gain from other parts of it. They also shouldn't criticize the whole book and prevent others from reaping the advantages of communicating with God that could be spoken of in the less offensive pages.

Let this book, whose aim is to teach people to talk with God, do all that it can. If I had found any volume that already said what I wanted, I would never have taken the trouble to write this or publish it. There are several good devotions, written by conformist and nonconformist ministers. These are excellent to instruct us in the content and language of prayer if we keep our spiritual freedom and do not tie our thoughts down to men's words. Henry's *Method for Prayer* and *Closet Devotions* are both valuable help for the humble and serious worshiper.

Those six sermons on prayer are the useful efforts of some of my closest friends, and they contain many righteous thoughts. But they take in the whole range of this subject, so there wasn't enough room to expand on what I intended.

Bishop Wilkins, in his sermon on the gift of prayer, has been my main assistant in the second chapter of this book. There are many writings I have consulted to gain a clearer understanding, including those of Dr. Owen and others who have written for or against the work of the Spirit in prayer. And I have also borrowed from the anonymous book with the fancy title, Generation of Seekers, in which several practical cases about the aids of the Spirit are handled well.

And if any advances are made beyond the efforts of great men gone past, I hope the world will justify this attempt. And if younger Christians reading this improve in the holy skill of prayer, when they get near to the throne of grace, may they pray that this book may carry on the good work of helping others in the work of praise.

Layout of the Book

Prayer is a word that has a broad meaning in the Bible. It is not just a request for mercies, but it represents the address of a person on earth to God in heaven about everything that concerns his God, his neighbor or himself, in this world or the world to come. It is the conversation that God allows us to have with Himself while we are here below. It is the language in which a person communicates with their Creator and in which the soul of a Christian often gets near to God, experiences great delight, and dwells with their heavenly Father for a short time before going to heaven. It is a wonderful privilege that our Maker has given us, as well as a necessary part of the obedience he requires from us in every circumstance of life.

- *"Pray without ceasing"* (1 Thess 5:17).
- *"In everything by prayer and supplication with thanksgiving let your requests be made known to God"* (Phil 4:6).
- *"Praying at all times in the Spirit, with all prayer and supplication"* (Eph 6:18).

Prayer is a part of divine worship that is required of all people and should be done with the voice or in the heart, called vocal or mental prayer. It is commanded of individuals in their personal lives, in a serious and consistent habit; and in the affairs of life, by secretly and suddenly lifting the heart up to God. It also belongs to communities, as families, corporations, parliaments, courts, or societies for trade and business; and to religious communities. When people meet for any godly purpose, they should seek God. It is especially required of churches because the house of God is the house of prayer.

Since it is a very necessary duty for everyone across the world, it is right that we should all know how to do it correctly, that it may be acceptable to God, and become a wonderful and rewarding exercise for our own hearts and those that join with us.

I will write about prayer in the following order

1. a duty of worship
2. performed by the gifts or abilities God has given us
3. with the exercise of our character, and
4. assisted by the Spirit of God.

My conclusion will be aimed at urging Christians to seek after this holy skill of conversation with God.

1

WHAT IS PRAYER?

When speaking about prayer as an act of worship, we can divide it into several parts to understand the whole essence of prayer better: calling on God, praise, confession, requests, pleading, declaration (or dedication), thanksgiving, and blessing. We will look at each one specifically.

Calling on God

The first part of prayer is invocation or calling on God. It can include these three things:

1. **Mentioning one or more of God's names or titles.** In this way, we indicate and acknowledge the person we pray to. There are many examples of this recorded in the Bible: "Lord my God, most high and most holy God and Father;" "God of Israel, who dwells among

the cherubim;" "Almighty God, the everlasting King;" "Our Father who is in heaven;" "God, that keeps the covenant;" and many others.

2. **A declaration of our desire to worship him.** "To you, we lift up our souls. We draw near to you as our God. We come into your presence. We are just dust and ashes and come to speak to your majesty. We bow before you in humble speech," or something like this. It would also be good to briefly mention how unworthy we are.

3. **A desire for his help and acceptance,** using language like this: "Lord, stir us up to call on your name. Assist us by your Spirit to access Your mercy seat. Raise our hearts towards you. Teach us to approach you, God of grace." *"Give attention to the sound of my cry, my King and my God, for to you do I pray"* (Psalm 5:2).

In these words, all three parts of calling on God are expressed.

Praise

The second part of prayer is praise or honor given to God by the created being. It contains these four things:

1. **A mention of his nature as God**, with the highest characteristics and perfections: His self-sufficient existence—He is God of and from himself; his unity of essence—there is no other God besides Him; His existence in three persons—the Father, the Son, and

the Holy Spirit, that is the mystery of the Trinity that is beyond our understanding.

How far above all creatures he is and his infinite superiority of nature should also be added here. The words used in this part, sound like this: "You are God, and there is none else, your name is Jehovah, the most high. Who in the heavens can be compared to the Lord, or who among the sons of the mighty is like our God? All the nations before you are like nothing, and in your eyes, they are counted as nothing and vanity. You are the first and the last, the only true and living God; your glorious name is exalted above all blessing and praise."

1. **The mention of his many attributes**, with expressions of praise, grace, and affection for his power, justice, wisdom, sovereignty, holiness, goodness, and mercy. There are a lot of these verses in the Bible that the saints have spoken to God: "You are very great, Lord, you are clothed with honor and majesty. You are the blessed and only potentate, King of kings, and Lord of lords. All things are naked and open before your eyes. You search the heart of man, but how unsearchable is your understanding, and your power is unknown. Your eyes are too pure to look at iniquity. Your mercy endures forever. You are slow to anger, abundant in goodness, and your truth reaches to all generations."

These meditations are useful at the beginning of our prayers, to bring us low before the throne of God, to awaken our reverence, dependence, faith and hope, humility, and joy.

1. **The mention of his many works**, of creation, providence, and grace, with adequate praises. Just as God is glorious in himself, his nature, and his attributes, so he has shown that glory to us by the works of his hands. And it is up to us to ascribe the same glory to him and tell him humbly that we are aware of the perfection of his works. We could say: "You, Lord, have made the heavens and the earth. The whole of creation is the work of your hands. You rule among the armies of heaven and among the inhabitants of the earth, and you do what pleases you. You have revealed your goodness towards mankind and have magnified your mercy. Your works of nature and grace are full of wonder."
2. **The mention of his relation to us** as a creator, father, redeemer, king, friend, and our eternal reward. And here it will be good to mention the name of Jesus, who brought us near to God to be made his children; by whose incarnation and atonement he becomes a God and Father to sinful men and appears their reconciled friend. And through him, we continue to draw nearer to God in every part of this praise.

When we consider his nature, we are just creatures before God, because he is infinitely superior to us. When we speak of his attributes, an acquaintance grows between God and us, as we tell him that we have learned something of his power, wisdom, justice, and mercy. But when we carry on and mention the works of his hands, by which he shows himself to us, we approach even nearer to God. And when we finally can call him our God, because of his relation to us in Jesus, then we gain access and are better prepared for the next parts of this worship.

Confession

The third part of prayer is confession. This can be divided into four points:

1. **A humble confession of our original nature**; our distance from God, as we are created beings; our subjection to him; and our constant dependence on him. "You, Lord, are in heaven, but we are on the earth; our being is but of yesterday, and our origin is in the dust. What is man that you are mindful of him, and the son of man that you should visit him? Man, that is a worm, and the son of man, that is but a worm! It is in you that we live, move, and have our being: you withhold your breath, and we die."
2. **A confession of our sins**: both original, which belong to our nature; and actual, that have been done in the course of our lives. We should confess our sins as we feel the guilt of them, as well as the deep, sad power of sin in our hearts. We should confess the sins that we have been guilty of in thought, as well as the iniquities of our mouths and our lives; our sins we do not know about and sins we willingly did; the

sins of our childhood and adult years; sins against the law of God and sins committed against the gospel of Jesus Christ.

Sometimes it is necessary to add specific details of our various mistakes and stupidities. We should mourn before God because of our pride and vanity; the intensity of our passions; our carnal thoughts and love of this world; the indulgence of our flesh; our earthly security and ingratitude under so many mercies, and our worry, impatience, or discouragement in times of trouble; our neglect and lack of love to God; our unbelief and hardness of heart; our laziness and in our belief; the dishonor we have brought to God; and all our failures towards other people.

And these may be intensified on purpose to humble our hearts even more before God by reflecting on them all: how often they have been repeated, before and since we knew God; that we have committed them against the light and have sinned against love; and we have committed these after many rebukes from the Bible, wisdom, and support from the gospel and the Spirit. This part of prayer is often insisted and emphasized among those examples in the Bible.

And with these confessions, we must grieve and feel our shame. "We are ashamed and embarrassed to lift our faces before you, God, because of the many iniquities that cover our head and trespasses that stretch so high. See, we are disgraceful; what can we say to you? We will lay our hands on our mouths and put them in the dust if it brings us any hope."

1. **A confession because we deserve punishment** for all our sins and do not deserve mercy. We can use words like these: "Lord, we deserve to be thrown out of your presence forever and to be eternally cut off from all hope of mercy. We deserve to fall under the curse of the law that we have broken and to be forever banished from the blessings of the gospel that we have refused for so long. We have sinned against so much mercy that we are no longer worthy to be called your children. We are not worthy of any favor promised in your Word that you have given us encouragement to hope for. If you challenge us on our transgressions, we cannot answer you, Lord, or make any excuses. If you should keep count of iniquities, who can stand? But there is forgiveness with you, there is mercy and redemption."
2. **A confession of our needs and hardships.** The specifics of this come under the next section, but it is necessary for them to be laid out before God in his presence because God loves to hear us tell him how we feel about our own needs and troubles. He loves to hear us complain before him when we are under any pressure from his hand or when we stand in need of mercies of any kind.

Requests

The fourth part of prayer is requests, which includes a desire to be delivered from evil and a request to receive good things. For both of these, we must offer our petitions to God for ourselves and other people.

The iniquity we pray to be delivered from is temporary, spiritual, or eternal. "Lord, take away the guilt of our sins by the atonement of your Son. Subdue the power of our iniquities by your Spirit. Deliver us from the natural darkness of our minds, from the corruption of our hearts, and perverse tendencies of our passions. Free us from the temptations that we are exposed to and the daily snares that trap us. We are in constant danger in this life, we need God to watch over us for our defense. Deliver us from your judgment and eternal punishment in hell because of our sins. Save us from the power of our enemies in this world and from all the painful evil that we have exposed ourselves to by sinning against you.'

The good we want to receive is also temporary, spiritual, or eternal. As we pray for the pardon of all our sins through atonement and our Redeemer's death, so we beg God for our justification through the righteousness of Jesus and our acceptance with God to eternal life. We pray for sanctification by his Holy Spirit, for him to teach us the knowledge of God in Jesus, as well as to reveal to us the evil of sin and its danger. We pray for the consolation of the Spirit, that he would not only bring faith, love, and every spiritual fruit in our hearts, but give us evidence of his work and our own interest in God's love.

We say to God, "You have the hearts of everyone in your hand; form our hearts according to your will and according to the image of your Son. Be our light and our strength; make us run in the ways of holiness. Give us grace that we may do what you have appointed for us. Preserve your gospel among us, and let all your ways be sanctified. Let your mercies draw us nearer to you with cords of love, and let your hand turn us from sin and deny the world, and make us ready to be with you whenever you call us. Guide us by your counsel; secure us by your grace as we travel through this dangerous wilderness and give us victory over death and a rich entry into your Son's glorious kingdom."

But while we are on earth, we have these human bodies, and there are many things we need to support us and make us comfortable; "We ask that you would give these things to us, in line with your glory and grace. Keep our health, strength, and peace, and let holiness be written on all of them so that whatever we receive from can be used for your honor. Heal our sicknesses and forgive our sins, that our hearts may bless you."

And as we are required to offer requests for ourselves and make them known to God, we are also commanded to pray for other Christians (Eph 6:18) and to intercede for all people (7 Tim 2:1). 'Intercession' is the common name for this type of request.

In general, we must pray for the church, for it is close to God's heart and is written on the palms of Jesus' hands. Its welfare should also be on our hearts; we should always have concern for the whole church in the world. He values his church above kingdoms and nations. Therefore, we should plead with God for his church more than for any nation, that he would increase the dominion of Christ; that he would spread his gospel among the lost and make the name of Jesus known and honored from the rising of the sun to its going down; that he would call in the remnant, the Jews; that he would bring the fullness of the Gentiles into his church; and that he would pour an abundant measure of his Spirit on us to carry out his own work on the earth.

And we must ask that the Spirit will come in great power on churches, ministers, families, and believers. We must pray that God delivers his church from the power of persecuting enemies and that he holds back the anger of man and does not allow the wicked to triumph over the righteous.

We must also ask for God's mercy for the country we are in, that freedom and peace may be established and flourish; for governments that rule over us; and that they will have wisdom and faithfulness to manage those affairs God has entrusted them with on earth.

We must pray for our friends and relatives, that God would deliver them from all the evil they feel or fear, and also give them all the good that we wish for ourselves on earth and in heaven.

There is also another kind of request which was often used in the Old Testament, and that is calling for vengeance and destruction on enemies. But this should seldom be used because the gospel is a covenant of love. It should never be used against our personal enemies, but only against those enemies of Jesus that are irreconcilable to him. Jesus taught us in his life, and gave us an example at his death, to forgive and pray for our enemies, for that is honorable and the glory of our faith.

Notice that when we pray for those things which are necessary for the glory of God or our own salvation, we can be more persistent in prayer. We can say "Lord, without forgiveness of our sins we cannot rest; without the renewal of our hearts by your grace, our souls can never rest; without the hope of heaven we can never be at peace, and we will never let you go until you bless us. For Zion's sake we will not be quiet, and for the sake of Jerusalem, your glory, your church in the world, we will not rest until you have made her the joy of the earth."

But, when we plead with God for those things that our salvation or his glory do not depend on, we should not be persistent in prayer but must learn to limit our requests like this: "If it is consistent with your ways, with the purposes of grace, and your glory, then give us this blessing. If it is in the interest of our hearts and for your honor, then let this favor be granted to us. Otherwise, we resign ourselves to your wisdom, and say, Father, not our will, but yours be done."

Pleading

The fifth part of prayer can be called pleading with God. This is not a distinct part by itself and belongs to the work request, but it is so very large and diffusive that it will be treated separately. Pleading with God, or arguing our case with him in a passionate yet humble manner, is one part of that persistence in prayer that the Bible recommends. This is what all the believers through the ages have practiced. This is what Job engages in: If I could get nearer to God, *"I would lay my case before him and fill my mouth with arguments"* (Job 23:3-4). This is what the prophet Jeremiah practices: *"Righteous are you, O Lord when I complain to you; yet I would plead my case before you. Why does the way of the wicked prosper?"* (Jer. 12:1). We cannot think our arguments will have any influence on God's will and persuade him to change his mind.

But as he talks with us in the way humans do, so he allows us to talk with him in the same manner and encourages us to plead with him as if he was really moved and persuaded by our persistence. So Moses is said to have persuaded God to preserve Israel when he seemed set on their destruction (Exod. 32:7—14). In pleading with God, there are many arguments, but the main ones can be put into the following topics:

1. **We can plead with God from the significance of our needs, dangers, or sorrows**, whether they relate to the soul or the body, to this life or the life to come, to ourselves or those for whom we pray. We can make our arguments for deliverance from the kind of trials that we suffer. "My sorrows, Lord, burden me and might make me dishonor your name and gospel. My pains and weaknesses stop me from serving you so that I am useless on earth and a burden to others. They have gone on for so long that I'm afraid I won't be able to hold out, or bear it in my spirit if your hand is heavy on me. If this sin is not taken away, or that temptation removed, I'm afraid I will be turned away from the faith and let go of my hope." So, from the type, degree, or duration of our difficulties, we can make our arguments for relief.
2. **The perfection of God** provides another argument in prayer: "For your mercies' sake, Lord, save me.

Your lovingkindness is infinite; let this infinite lovingkindness be seen in my salvation. You are wise, Lord; though my enemies are crafty, you can disrupt their schemes, and you know how to turn my sorrows into joy. You can bring me an escape when everyone else stands back and cannot see any way to help me. You are almighty and all-sufficient; your power can overcome my opponents, defeat the devil, break the powers of darkness, release me from the chains of my corruption, and bring me into freedom. You are just and righteous; will you let the enemy oppress me forever? You are sovereign, and all things are at your command. You can say to pains and diseases, 'Go or come'; so, speak the sovereign word of healing, and my body and soul will praise you. You delight in forgiving grace; it is the honor of our God to forgive. Therefore, let my iniquities be canceled through the abundance of your rich mercy."

3. **God's relation to humans, particularly to his own people** is the next argument that can be used. "Lord, you are my Creator; do not you treasure the work of your hands? Haven't you made and fashioned me, and will you now destroy me? You are my king; to whom should I go to for protection but you, when the enemies of your honor and my soul surround me? Aren't you my father, and haven't you called me your child and given me a name and a place among your sons and daughters? Why should I look like one that has been thrown out or one who belongs to the family of Satan? Haven't you got the heart of a father and compassion? Why should one of your poor,

weak, helpless children be neglected or forgotten? Aren't you my God in covenant, and the God and Father of my Lord Jesus Christ, by whom that covenant is guaranteed? Under that relation, I plead with you for all necessary mercies."

4. **The different promises of the covenant of grace** form another class of arguments to use in prayer. "Teach me, Lord, and forgive me, and sanctify my soul. Give me grace and glory according to your promise that caused me to hope. Remember your word in heaven; it is recorded in your covenant that I must receive light, love, strength, joy, and happiness. Aren't you a faithful God to fulfill every one of those promises? What if heaven and earth pass away? does not your covenant stand on two immovable pillars—your promise and oath? Now I have run to grab hold of this hope; let me have your help. Remember the covenant made with your Son in eternity, and let the mercies that were promised to his seed be given to me according to my various needs." Recalling the covenant of God has often been very successful and effective in the prayers of the believers.

5. **The name and honor of God before people** is another powerful argument. *"For the Canaanites and all the inhabitants of the land will hear of it and will surround us and cut off our name from the earth. And what will you do for your great name?"* (Josh. 7:9). If your people die in multitudes, who will still praise you on earth? *"Death does not praise you…the living, he thanks you, as I do this day."* This was the pleading of Hezekiah (Isaiah 38:18—19). And David uses the same language in Psalm

6:5. "For your name's sake" was a mighty argument in all the ancient times of the church.

6. **Former experiences** are also arguments to make use of in prayer. Jesus is represented in that prophetic psalm using this argument: *"In you our fathers trusted; they trusted, and you delivered them. To you they cried and were rescued; in you they trusted and were not put to shame"* (Psalm 22:4-5). "Let me be a part of the same favor while I cry to you and trust you. You have never said to the seed of Jacob, Seek my face in vain, and it won't be said that your poor servant has now looked for your face and not found you. Often I have received mercy in response to prayer. Often my soul has drawn near to you and been comforted in times of sorrow. Often I have taken fresh grace according to my need from the grace that is in Christ. Shall the door of these treasures be closed to me now? Shall I receive no more favor from God's hand, who has given so abundantly to me before?"

However improper this sort of argument may seem in court, or to gain favor with great men, God loves to hear his own people make use of it. The more we receive from God, if we humbly acknowledge him, the more we are likely to receive.

1. **The name and mediation of Jesus** is the most powerful argument. There are some hints of it in the Old Testament, but it was never taught so clearly until just before he left this world: *"Until now you have asked nothing in my name. Ask, and you will receive, that your joy may be full"* (John 16:24-23). This seems to be

> reserved for prayer under the gospel. We are taught to mention the name of Jesus, the only begotten and eternal Son of God, as a method to receive our biggest requests and fullest salvation.

This is the language we should use when addressing the Father: "Lord, let my sins be forgiven, for the sake of your love for your own Son; for the sake of his love for you; for the sake of his humbling himself as a human to look like a sinner and be made a sacrifice, even though he was free from sin; for the sake of his perfect and painful obedience, which has honored your law; for the sake of the curse he took on himself and the death he suffered, which glorified your authority and honored your justice more than the depth of my sins. Remember his dying cry; remember his agonies when darkness was on him, and do not let the powers of darkness cover me. Remember the day when you stood back from your own Son as he cried as being forsaken of God, and let me have your everlasting presence with me. Let me never be forsaken, since your Son has taken that punishment."

Again, we may plead with God the intercession of Jesus, our High Priest above: "Father, we ask for nothing but what your Son already asks you for. We request nothing from your hands but what your own Son requests for us. Look on the Lamb, as he has been slain; look on his pure and perfect righteousness and that blood with which our High Priest entered into the heavens, and in which he appears forever before you to make intercession. Let every blessing be given to me that his blood purchased and which he pleads for at your right hand. What can you deny your own Son? For he has told us that you always hear him. For the sake of the Son you love, do not deny us."

Declaration

The sixth part of prayer consists of a declaration or dedication.

This is very seldom mentioned as a part of prayer, but it seems so necessary and distinct from all the rest that it should be treated separately. It can be divided into these four points:

1. **A declaration of our relationship to God.** It is worthwhile for a Christian to draw near to God and tell him that he is the Lord's; that he belongs to his family; that he is one of his household; that he stands as one of his children; that his name is written in his covenant. There is a lot of spiritual delight and satisfaction that comes from telling God of our relation to him.
2. **A declaration of our previous transactions with God.** "Lord, we have given ourselves to you and chosen you for our eternal portion and our highest good. We have seen the insufficiency of created beings to make us happy, and we have aligned ourselves to a higher hope. We have seen Jesus the Saviour in his righteousness and grace. We have put our trust in him, and we have made our covenant with the Father, by the sacrifice of his Son. We have drawn near to you in your laws. We have confirmed

the covenant at your communion table, as well our devotion to you through the act of baptism. We have given our names to God in his house, and we have chosen to be the Lord's."

3. **A surrender of ourselves to God and a declaration of our love towards him**. This is sweet language in prayer when the heart is in the right place. "Lord, I confirm my dedication of myself and my covenant with you. If I was not sincere before in giving myself up, I do it now from the bottom of my heart. I commit my guilty heart into Jesus' hands, that he may sprinkle it with his atoning blood, that he may cover it with his justifying righteousness and make me, a sinner, accepted in the presence of a just and holy God. I come into the presence of your justice and holiness, clothed by your own Son, and I trust you see no sin in me to punish. I give my heart, that is corrupt and sinful by nature, into the hands of my almighty Savior, that by his grace he may renew it; that he may suppress every bad appetite and root out every selfish passion; that he may form me after his own image, fill me with his grace, and fit me for his glory."

"I hope in you, my God, for you are my refuge, strength, and salvation. I love you above all things, and I know I love you. Who else do I have in heaven but you? There is no one on earth that compares to you. I desire you with my strongest affections, and I delight in you above all delights. My soul stands in awe and fear before you; and I rejoice to love such an almighty, revered God."

1. **A declaration of our humble decision to be the Lord's forever.** This is what is generally called a vow. I do not encourage Christians to frequently make the same vows, especially in ordinary things; this often proves to be a dangerous trap for people. But we can surrender our hearts to God and vow to be the Lord's forever often: to love him above all things, to fear him, to hope in him, to walk in his ways in obedience, and to wait for his mercy to eternal life. This kind of vow is included in baptism and the Lord's Supper. It is comprehended in almost every act of worship, and especially in serious prayer to God.

Lastly, together with declaration or dedication to God, it is necessary that we renounce everything inconsistent with this: "I am yours, Lord, and I do not belong to this world. I have given myself to you, and I have turned away from sin and from the flesh. I have renounced the world and chosen the Father. I have renounced all other saviors and my own righteousness in favor of God and chosen Jesus as my only way to the Father. I have renounced my own strength as my only hope; because my understanding is dark, my will is weak, and my best attempts are insufficient to get me to heaven. I renounce my dependence on all of them, that I may receive light, strength, and love from God. I am dead to the law and sin, I am crucified to the world by the cross of Jesus my Savior. I tell Satan to get behind me; I renounce him and his works. I will not fear him nor love him, nor be yoked with people of this world, for I love and fear my God, and in him is my eternal help and hope. What have I got to do with idols anymore? I will banish the objects of temptation from my sight. I leave everything that would divide me from God, to whom I have surrendered myself.

And if you see fit to discipline and correct me, I submit to your hand, God. If you deny my requests I have brought you, I leave myself in your hands, trusting you to choose better for me. And because I know the weakness of my heart and the inconstancy of my will, I humbly put all these, my vows, into Jesus' hands to fulfill them in and by me, through all my days."

Thanksgiving

The seventh part consists of thanksgiving. To give thanks is to acknowledge the hand that gives us our blessings and to give honor and praise to the power, wisdom, and goodness of God. And this is part of that tribute which God our king expects for everything we receive from him. It is terrible for a created being to accept benefits from God, and then forget his heavenly benefactor. Our thanksgivings may be arranged under two points: we must give thanks for those benefits we have prayed for, and for those that God has given without us praying for them.

1. **Those blessings that God has given us without our asking** should be mentioned first because they are the effects of his rich mercy. How many blessings of his goodness with which he has presented us! "We praise you, Lord, for your original design of love to fallen man, that you should make a distinction between us and the angels that sinned. What is man,

that you are mindful of his salvation and allow the angels to perish forever without rescue; that you choose a certain number of the human race, and give them into Jesus' hands before all worlds and make a covenant of grace with them in Jesus, that their joy might be secured; that you should reveal this mercy in promises to our fathers by the prophets and that in your appointed time you sent your Son to take on our nature, and redeem us by his death?"

"We give glory to your justice and grace for this work of terror and compassion, reconciling sinners to yourself by the punishment of your Son. We praise you for the gospel you have brought to the world, the gospel of forgiveness and peace, that you confirmed by many testimonies to raise and establish our faith. We give glory to your power that has guarded the gospel through the ages, against Satan's opposition, and proclaimed the good news of peace in our nation."

"We bless you for coming to live amongst us, that we should be born in a land of light. What a favor that among all your creation we should be placed above all other beings; but even more that we should be born of believing parents under the promises of grace. We give thanks for keeping us from many dangers that we never see coming and which we cannot ask you to prevent. How indebted we are to you, Lord, that you have not cut us off because of our flesh and sin, and that our reward is not as children of damnation; that we have so many conveniences and comforts given to us, as well as grace; and all this before we even knew you or looked for any your mercies!"

1. **We must give thanks for the blessings we have received** as an answer to prayer. Whatever we have asked God for demands our acknowledgment of his goodness when we receive it. There is no need to list specifics because we can look back at the fourth part of prayer, requests, and read about our gratitude. We will learn to give glory to God for being delivered from temporary and spiritual evil, and our hope of being delivered from eternal evil; for the good given to our heart and body and our expectation of eternal joy for both; for mercies on the churches, on countries and governments, on our relatives and friends, as well as ourselves. And we should rejoice and say to the Lord, "Truly you are a God that hears prayer, and you have not despised the cry of those that looked for you. We are witnesses that you did not call your people to seek your face in vain."

All our thanksgivings can be brought in prayer by remembering the mercies we have received; by mentioning the glory and self-sufficiency of God the giver; that he is happy in himself and has no need of us, and yet he wants to bless us; that he is sovereign and could remove his favor to thousands and leave us out of his chosen. We are as wicked and unworthy as others, and our God sees all our unworthiness, guilt, repeated sins, mercies abused, and yet he continues to have mercy on us and to be gracious.

Blessing

The eighth part is the blessing of God, which is slightly different from praise or adoration, and also from thanksgiving. In Psalm 145:10 it says, *"All your works shall give thanks to you, O Lord, and all your saints shall bless you!"* Even the inanimate creation, which are God's works, show his character and his praises, but his people do something more—they bless his name. This part of worship consists of two things:

1. **Mentioning the many attributes and glories of God** with joy and pleasure. "We delight to see your name honored in the world, and we rejoice in your excellence. We take pleasure seeing you exalted above all. We triumph in the perfections of your nature, and we give thanks when we think of your holiness." So, we rejoice and bless the Lord for what he is, as well as for what he has done for us. This is a divine and unselfish act of worship.
2. **Wishing the glories of God may continue forever**, and rejoicing at the confidence of it. "May the name of God be blessed forever; may the kingdom, the power, and the glory be ascribed to him forever; may all generations call him honorable and make his name glorious in the earth. To you, Father, Son, and Holy Spirit belong everlasting power and honor"

Amen

We are taught in many verses to finish our prayers with Amen, which is a Hebrew word meaning truth or faithfulness, certainly, surely, etc. It implies four things:

1. **A belief** of all that we have said concerning God and ourselves, of giving honor to God by mentioning his name, attributes, and works; and a persuasion of our own unworthiness, needs, and sorrows which we have already expressed.
2. **A desire** to gain all that we have prayed for, longing after it and looking for it. "Lord, let it be as we have said" is the language of this little word Amen, at the end of our prayers.
3. **A confirmation** of all our declarations, promises, and engagements to God. It is used as the promise of God in some verses: *"Surely I will bless you"* (Heb. 6:13-14). It is a promise in our lips, binding ourselves to the Lord according to the declarations we have made in the previous part of worship.
4. **The hope and expectation** of the acceptance of us and our prayers. For while we confirm our dedication of ourselves to God, we also humbly lay claim to his accomplishment of the promises of his covenant, and expect and wait that he will fulfill all our requests in line with his own glory.

Study Guide

Without trying to add or take away from what Watts has already mentioned on the nature of prayer, this study guide simply creates a space to think about what you have just read and how it applies to your own life, especially in the area of praying. Take your time to work through the questions. You don't have to complete all of them, or even follow the order, but rather allow them to lead you to think, reflect, and hear from the Spirit what needs to change or be given more attention.

In this chapter, instead of just explaining the concept of prayer, it is dissected into its many parts. At first, it may seem like a strict pattern to follow, but as we look at each of the segments, we will realize that they form a natural, logical order that begins with exclaiming who God is, working toward our own confessions and requests, then remembering all that has been done for us, before concluding. As a helpful format, it can bring us into the correct frame of mind when we want to pray.

1. In your own words, how would you describe prayer?
2. Do you ever begin your prayers by 'calling on God,' acknowledging who he is and how much you need his help? Do you start with praising him or do you rush in to ask and plead for things?
3. Why do you think it is important to begin the way Watts describes?
4. Notice that confession also comes before requests and pleading. What do you think is the benefit of

doing it in this order?
5. Which of these parts of prayer are you really good at? Which ones do you struggle with? Do you often completely leave some of them out? Why?
6. Have you ever thought that there is more to saying "Amen" at the end of a prayer than just as a way to show you are finished?
7. How would you describe your personal prayer life? If you had to rate it, what score would you give it out of 10?

2
THE GIFT OF PRAYER

Having spoken about the nature of prayer and its several parts, we now look at the gift or ability to pray.

This skill of speaking to God in prayer has usually been called a gift. Some have mistakenly gone on to see it as being like the gift of miracles or prophecy, which are God-given, completely out of our reach, and unattainable by our efforts. Following this, others have slammed the view of it as a gift as nothing more than unfounded and crazy.

But I will attempt to give a rational account of it in the following sections and lay down clear suggestions on how to attain it with the help of the Holy Spirit. I hope this will remove the confusion and the criticism.

What Is the Gift of Prayer?

The gift of prayer can be described as the ability to adapt our thoughts to all the parts and designs of it, and a readiness to express those thoughts before God in a manner that will profit our own souls as well as the souls of others that join us.

It is called a gift, partly because it was given to the early Christians in a sudden and extraordinary manner by the Spirit, and partly because the help of the Spirit is required to attain this skill or ability to pray.

In the first spread of the gospel, the Spirit of God gave various powers and abilities to the believers, and these were called the gifts of the Spirit (1 Cor. 12:4, 8-9). These were the gifts of preaching, exhortation, making and singing psalms, healing the sick, speaking in tongues, etc. Now, though these were given instantly in an extraordinary way back then, and divine power made it possible to use them, these powers or abilities to speak in tongues, of psalmody, of preaching and healing, are to be obtained by human diligence, depending on the blessing of God. The same must be said concerning the gift of prayer.

As the art of medicine or healing is founded on the knowledge of natural principles and is made up of rules drawn from the nature of things and reason and observation, so the art of preaching is learned and attained by the knowledge of divine principles and the use of rules and suggestions for explaining and applying divine truths. So, the skill of prayer is built on a knowledge of God and ourselves and can be taught as a logical method using proper suggestions and rules. But, because we expect the aid of the Holy Spirit in things so serious and holy, the skill of preaching and praying are still called the gifts of the Spirit.

Types of Prayer

The gift of prayer is one of the most honorable and useful in the Christian life and should be sought with desire and diligence. In order to attain it, we must avoid these two extremes:

1. *Only Using Pre-Composed Prayers*

It is convenient and better for weaker Christians to use a structure in prayer rather than not pray at all. Jesus seems to have done this for his disciples in their early days of Christianity (Luke 1 1:1-13). Sometimes the most mature Christians can find their needs, desires, and the state of their hearts better expressed in other people's words than they could do it themselves. In a holy manner, they could use those words, especially when they are experiencing dryness of spirit or struggling in this area. Much help can be borrowed by younger and elder Christians from prayers that are well written, without using the whole form as a prayer. Someone else said, "forms may be useful, and in some cases necessary."

We say this because

1. Some people are so uneducated and ignorant that they cannot properly express their desires in prayer—must they give up praying? Is it not better in their ignorance to use others' works and writings than not to pray at all, or to say something useless and unholy? This is not to excuse their ignorance, nor to encourage them to stay in that condition, but to help them where they are.
2. Some use this form privately, which might be fine in their personal prayer to God; but when they pray before others, they lack the ability to express themselves or the confidence to do so. I cannot excuse this sinful shyness.
3. It is possible that some physical impairment or sudden distraction might cloud their minds, weaken their memories, and dull their senses so that they cannot express themselves spontaneously. This can happen in case of depression, temporary spasm or stroke, or similar disorders.

In cases like these, a form of prayer can be useful and helpful. It is not tying up the Spirit if it is mindfully used, and with the Spirit's assistance will find acceptance with God. However, this is not a license to only use written forms of prayer, especially for those who can pray but are forced by others to do so. If ignorance, shyness, bad memory, or other disorder makes it necessary for some to use, is it right for everyone else to do the same? How can we ever desire better gifts? Why should those that are gifted in praying be stopped from using it because others lack it?

Now, although the use of formal prayer in these cases is acceptable, constant use of them will bring difficulties like these:

1. **It restricts the free exercise of our own thoughts and desires**, which is the main function of prayer—to express our desires to God. Where our thoughts and affections should direct our words, now a set structure of words directs our thoughts and affections. If we bind ourselves only to those words, we dampen our devotion and prevent the holy fire from kindling our hearts. We discourage our active passion from following divine subjects, and we obstruct our souls from breathing towards heaven.

"The heart knows its own bitterness, and no stranger shares its joy" (Prov. 14:10). There are secret joys and unknown bitterness that the heart longs to bring before God and it cannot find the exact and corresponding expressions in the best prayer books. Must Christians suppress all those thoughts, and never allow that sweet conversation with God, because it is not written down in some book?

1. **The holy thoughts and emotions of the heart are formed in us by the Spirit**. If we do not express them because they are not found in prayer-books, we are in danger of resisting and quenching the Holy Spirit, and fighting against the plans of God for us—that we are warned against (1 Thess. 5:19) and which a humble Christian should be wary of.

2. **It cramps and imprisons those powers that God has given us for improvement and use.** It silences our natural abilities and does not allow them to act; it restricts our spiritual senses and prevents their growth. To be satisfied with simple books and liturgies, to confine ourselves to them and never use our own gifts, is spiritual laziness that should not be tolerated. It is hiding a talent in the earth that God has given us for trading with heaven. It is an abuse of our knowledge of divine things to neglect the use of it in our communication with God. It is as if a man that had once used crutches to support him when he was weak would always use them; or because he has found his own thoughts expressed by another person, will agree to what that other person always says, and never speak his own thoughts.
3. **It leads us into danger of hypocrisy and lip service.** Sometimes we will be tempted to express those things that are not the thoughts of our own hearts, and use words not suited to our needs, sorrows, or requests, because those words are put together beforehand.
4. **It can make our spirits cold, flat, and mechanical in our devotion,** even though it is not always done mechanically or without thinking. The constant repetition of the same words does not awaken the same feelings in our hearts, which they may have done when they were first written. When we continually walk one road of sentences or expressions, they become like an old beaten path that we travel and walk on every day without noticing

things along the way; so in our daily repetition of a form, we neglect proper attention to the full meaning of the words.

There is something better to awaken the mind in a formulated prayer when a Christian is making his own way toward God according to the situation of his heart and the urgency of his needs. To use the words of a writer, "While we are clothing the sense of our hearts in fit expressions and, as it were, digging the content of our prayers out of our own feelings and experiences, it keeps the heart closer at work."

1. **Prayer reveals to us the state of our own spirits.** But constant use of forms will restrict our knowledge of ourselves and prevent us from getting to know our own hearts, which is a huge advantage in maintaining our belief and faith. Daily observation of our own spirits will teach us where we are lacking and how to bring our prayers to God. But if we tie ourselves down to the same words, our own observation of our hearts will be of little use, since we must say the same expressions, whatever the state of our hearts may be. Just as an inner search of our souls and intimate acquaintance with ourselves is a way to obtain the gift of prayer, so the exercise of the gift of prayer will promote this self-acquaintance, which is discouraged and restricted by books, forms, and liturgy.

Lastly, I mention the most common, evident, and convincing argument against confining ourselves to a form. It leaves our conversation with God very imperfect. Formatted prayers can't be perfectly suited to all our spiritual states or occasions in life. Our circumstances are always changing. We have new sins to be confessed, new temptations and sorrows to be represented, new needs to be supplied. Every change in the affairs of a country, a family, or a person, requires suitable requests and acknowledgments. No prescribed composition can ever provide properly for all of these.

I admit, all our concerns of the heart and body can be included in some large and general form of words, which may be suitable to one time, place, or condition and not another. But generalities are cold and do not affect us, others, or those whose case should be represented before God. It is much sweeter for our hearts and to our fellow Christians to have our fears, doubts, complaints, temptations, and sorrows represented in the most exact and specific expressions, in a language the heart can feel when the words are spoken.

Now, though we often find pre-composed prayers that express our present circumstance, the gift of prayer is much better than any form, just as a skill in preaching is to be preferred to any pre-composed sermon; as a perfect knowledge in medicine is better than any recipes; or as a recipe to make a medicine is preferable to an off-the-shelf medicine. If you always read printed sermons, you will not gain the art of preaching; and the person who deals only in recipes shall never become a skillful doctor; nor can the gift of prayer be attained by constant confinement to forms.

Perhaps a stronger impression can be made by showing the cure of confinement to forms and bias against the gift of prayer. A bishop of the Church of England said this on the matter: "In the use of such prescript forms to which a man has been accustomed, he should be narrowly watchful over his own heart, for fear of that lip-service and formality which in such cases we are more especially exposed to. For anyone to set down and satisfy himself with his book-prayer, or some prescript form, and to go no further, is still to remain in his infancy and not to grow up in his new nature. This would be as if a man who once needed crutches should always make use of them afterward, and so remain in continual impotency.

Prayer by the book is usually something flat and dead, floating for the most part in generalities, and not particular enough for each occasion. There is no life and vigor in it to engage the affections as when it proceeds immediately from the soul itself and is the natural expression of those particulars of which we are most sensitive. It is not easy to express what a vast difference a man may find, in respect of inner comfort and satisfaction, between those personal prayers that are conceived from the affections, and those prescribed forms which we say by rote or read out of books" (Bishop Wilkins in his *Gift of Prayer*).

1. *Only Using Spontaneous Ideas and Suggestions*

Another extreme to be avoided is having no preparation for prayer and depending completely on sudden feelings and suggestions—as if we expected the intuition of the Holy Spirit on our minds as it was with the apostles and inspired saints; as though we relied on his continual impulses in the content, manner, and words of prayer, without any thought, care, or premeditation of our own.

It is true that when we have premeditated the content and method of our prayer exactly, we should not restrict ourselves from checking any holy desires that may arise in our hearts during devotion. It is good to learn the skill of praying and to prepare also by meditation, reading, or holy conversation, to exercise this gift.

Some people imagine that if they use no form, they must always pray spontaneously, or without any premeditation, and think that all free or conceived prayer is improvised. But these things need to be distinguished.

Conceived or free prayer is when the words of our prayer are not formed beforehand to direct our thoughts, but we conceive the substance first in our minds, and then put those concepts into words and expressions we think are best. This may be achieved by meditation before we begin to speak in prayer, being conscious of our thoughts and expressions.

Spontaneous prayer is when, without any reflection or meditation before, we address God and speak the thoughts of our hearts as fast as we think them. This is suitable for sudden, short prayers when we lift up our hearts to God in rapid requests or thanksgiving during our busy day-to-day lives. There are also other occasions for this kind of spontaneous prayer:

1. In personal prayer, the same degree of premeditation is not necessary, as in public. For we can have more freedom to express our thoughts and desires as they

come to us, which can be significant in stirring up and maintaining our own emotions, though this might not be decent and acceptable in public.

2. People who are naturally skilled, have lively characters or are good with words, are spiritually-minded, or are very experienced in prayer, are not bound to premeditate everything about prayer in their family devotions. Ministers whose characters and talents have been well developed are also not obliged to think over all the substance of every public prayer to God beforehand. A short reflection can give enough content for Christians who are capable and skilled. Bishop Wilkins tells us, "The proportion of gifts that a man has received is the measure of his work and duty in this case." But for serious and great occasions, public and private, when times are set apart for prayer, regular premeditation is very useful and advantageous to everyone.

3. There may be times that demand sudden conversations with God even from those who have little skill and experience, and they can rely on special help from the Spirit while they obey the call to pray.

But I suspect that some people who are not very skilled in praying and still have much to say against premeditation, are spiritually lazy as they turn away from anything that resembles a formulated prayer.

The arguments that may encourage younger Christians to prepare their thoughts for prayer beforehand are these:

1. **The common logic of man and nature teaches us** that something so serious and important, that requires care to perform properly, cannot be done without some forethought. The skill of a Christian in his heart is to be learned and improved by forethought and diligence; even more so in the public performance of it. Now if nature points us to it, and the Bible does not forbid it, why should we not pursue it? The words of Scripture seem to encourage premeditation, when they tell us we should not be impulsive with our mouth or hasty in our heart to say anything before God (Eccles. 5:2).

2. **The heart should be prepared for prayer**, because it is frequently spoken of in the Bible. But the heart cannot be prepared for any act of worship without some degree of premeditation. What is the use of reading the Bible just before prayer in our families? Why are we often advised to think about the sermons we hear when we pray, except that by premeditation we may be better equipped?

3. **There is no such thing as learning to pray regularly without it.** The division of the nature of prayer into several parts—praise, confession, requests—is useless if we must not think before it. The rules that ministers give to teach us to pray are nothing if we do not have to think beforehand. If we do not consider our sins, needs, or mercies before we pray, there is no possibility of learning to perform this part of Christian worship with any decency or profit. Avoiding thinking beforehand, for whatever

reason, will block you from achieving the gift of prayer to any reasonable degree.

4. **Preparation for prayer is the way to serve God with our best.** For younger Christians who are unskilled, to always rush into the presence of God in prayer without forethought even when there is time to do so and to pour out words before God in any direction, shows a lack of reverence which they owe to the One before whom angels cover their faces, and who is jealous of his own worship and hates the sacrifice of fools.

If we completely neglect preparation, we will be ready to fall into many difficulties. Sometimes there will be long and awkward gaps in prayer, not knowing what to say next. At other times we shall be in danger of saying things that are off point, and wander far, which can never be acceptable to God. And sometimes, when the mind is not equipped, we run into a confused, incoherent jumble of words, that dishonors God, and edifies no one, especially us. The Spirit of God stands back from us for a season; perhaps to rebuke our negligence of learning to pray.

Bad practices like these have been an offense to those sincere Christians and a stumbling block and scandal to those causing division. The world has found a reason to criticize all conceived prayer, under the name of praying spontaneously and has tried to make all prayer without books and forms as offensive as possible.

The more clear-thinking part of the Church of England, which usually worships God by liturgies and pre-composed forms, has been too keen to listen to the criticisms and has used them to confirm their attachment to liturgies and prayer-books. They have been hardened against seeking the gift of prayer and oppose and censure those who have it. This public scandal can be found among those few bold, ignorant, and careless men who have been guilty of such impulsive and thoughtless prayers to God, pretending to do so by the Spirit.

In opposition to premeditation, some Christians may say, "I have meditated on many things that I wanted to say in prayer, but when I came to pray, my thoughts were too many and got carried away to other subjects and requests than what I had originally intended." Now I would persuade that person to receive this divine help, not to neglect premeditation in the future, but as a reward for their diligence in preparing their heart beforehand.

Another Christian will tell me that sometimes when they thought about things for prayer, they became confused between what was prepared and what they were feeling as opposed to if they had just prayed spontaneously. In reply, I must confess that I have sometimes had the same experience, but I blame it on one of three things:

1. Either my premeditation was superficial and imperfect in the content or method, so that the subjects of my prayer were not in any settled form and order in my memory, but were as uncertain as to the new thoughts that occur while praying. It is harder to fix something imperfect than to make something entirely new.

2. Or perhaps my premeditation had been all in my head, without any consultation of the state of my heart. I had prepared my head but not my heart for prayer. And then it is no wonder that when the heart comes to engage in prayer, it runs far from the premeditations of the head, and sometimes creates confusion in the mind.
3. Or it may be that my heart has not been in the right spirit and reluctant for prayer, and then I cannot blame premeditation; the prayer would have been as bad or worse without it.

But where the preparation of both head and heart was done carefully and wisely, I have experienced its usefulness, especially in my younger years, and on some extraordinary and serious occasions.

Finally, if some people have conscientiously and diligently attempted this way, and find they always pray more usefully and honorably, with more regularity and delight, by preparing the heart, without fixing the parts and method of their prayer in their mind beforehand, they must follow those methods of devotion that they have found most effective. But they must not block others from using premeditation, whom God has owned and approved in that way.

Few Christians become so effective and regular in the gift of prayer without learning premeditation. There are many more who are mediocre in this area because they do not think before it.

The Content of Prayer

First, it is necessary to have proper content so that we can converse with God; to keep our hearts and others focused in worship; to exercise our character and those of others by divine thoughts and desires in prayer; that we won't have long, awkward pauses while doing so or stop as soon as we have begun, because we lack content, or say far too many words to cover up the superficial meaning because there is so little real spiritual thought.

Therefore, I propose some rules to help give us proper content for prayer, and after that, will give some advice and suggestions concerning these materials of prayer.

Rules for Giving Prayer Content

Rule 1: Familiarize yourself with as many things that relate to Christianity as possible, for everything that relates to it can make up some part of the content of our prayer.

This is the most general and most universal rule that can be given here. Let us always be on the lookout for more extensive knowledge of God and ourselves. An acquaintance with God in his nature, people, perfection, works, and in His Word will supply us with plenty of subject matter for calling on God, praise, thanksgiving, and blessing. It will give us many arguments in pleading with God for mercy. An intimate knowledge of ourselves; our spirit, needs, sorrows, and joys will also supply us with proper thoughts for confession, requests, and giving thanks. We should get to know the Word of God to a greater degree, for there he reveals himself to us and also us to ourselves. Let the Scripture live in you with wisdom that you may be equipped with requests and praises.

We should also be observers of the way God deals with us in every way and know the state of our hearts well. We should observe the working of our hearts toward God and towards others, bring ourselves to account often, and examine our temper and our life in our natural, civil, and religious surroundings. For this purpose, it will be an advantage to keep a written record of God's provision as well as moments of his anger or mercy towards us.

Such observations and remarks in our daily walk with God will be a treasury to provide us with content for requests and praise. This is what the verse means when it talks of watching unto prayer (Eph. 6:18, 1 Pet. 4:7). This will make us ready to say something to God in prayer, concerning both him and ourselves. Let our judgments be solid and our characters and affections be passionate, then proper content will naturally rise and flow with ease and pleasure.

Rule 2: Let the nature of prayer, divided into its several parts, be ingrained in our hearts and our memories.

Let us always remember these several parts of worship: calling on God, praise, confession, requests, pleading, declaration, thanksgiving, and blessing. That we may remember them better, they can be summed up in these four lines:

Call on God, praise, confess,

Request, plead and then declare

You are the Lord's, give thanks and bless,

And let Amen confirm the prayer.

By remembering these parts of prayer, we will be assisted to improve in the performance of this part of worship.

It would help if people could write all these parts of prayer and all the related verses, or write down passages that we hear spoken in prayer that touch our hearts. This would preserve the thoughts and expressions that have motivated us. Bishop Wilkins, in his *Treatise of Prayer*, has given us collections of Scripture like this; and Mr. Henry has written down many more, arranged neatly under their proper subjects.

Rule 3: If you wish to have lots of material, do not be content with generalizations, but go into the specifics of your confessions, requests, and thanksgiving.

Consider the characteristics, glories, graces, and relations of God. Express your sins, needs, and sorrows, knowing the sad circumstances of each one. It will enlarge your hearts with prayer and humiliation if you confess the specifics and guilt of your sins—whether they've been committed against knowledge, against the warnings of conscience, etc. It will give you so much to be thankful for if you go over the wonderful times of mercy and comfort—that they are great, spiritual, and eternal, as well as temporary; that they were granted before you asked for them, or as soon as you asked, etc. And let your requests and your thanksgiving be suitable to where you are, who you are praying with, and those that you pray for.

Our burdens, cares, needs, and sins are many; so are our mercies and hopes; so are the attributes of God, his promises, and grace. If we open our mouths wide, he will fill and satisfy us with good things, according to his Word. If generalizations were sufficient for us, one short form would be enough to express ourselves to God in this manner: "Lord, you are great and good, but we are terrible sinners. Give us the mercies we need for the sake of Jesus Christ; and through him, accept all our thanksgivings for whatever we have and hope for. To the Father, Son, and Holy Spirit, be eternal glory. Amen."

This is a very general and comprehensive prayer that includes everything necessary in it. But no Christian can satisfy their soul, going to the mercy-seat every day, and just say this. A believer in the right state loves to pour out their heart before God in hundreds of details, and God expects his children to acknowledge their own special needs and his mercies, and to take notice of the smaller as well as the more obvious circumstances surrounding them. Let us not be confined, because God's hand and his heart are not confined. Jesus wants us to ask, and promises it will be given (Matt. 7:7). Paul tells us in everything by prayer and supplication to make known our requests to God (Phil. 4:6). And James tells us that we do not receive because we do not ask (James 4:2).

<u>Rule 4:</u> To give us content for prayer, it is convenient to read from the Bible or some Christian book, talk to fellow Christians about spiritual things, or spend time meditating on issues relating to Christianity.

This won't just supply us with content but will keep our thoughts on spiritual matters. Just before we start work, we should take time out from the world so that our spirits can converse with God. We can borrow content for prayer from what we read, from reflections of our own hearts, or church meetings. Many Christians have found that while he meditated, the fire burned inside of him (Psalm 39:3). And while we speak to others about spiritual issues, we will certainly find something to say to God.

Rule 5: If our hearts are dry and we find it difficult to pray before God, it is useful to take a book in our hand which contains some spiritual devotions, holy reflections, or patterns of prayer—the Psalms, the prophecies of Isaiah, the Gospels, or any of the Epistles.

So, we can lift up our hearts to God in short requests, praise, or thanksgiving, according to the verses or passages we read. We can call this mixed prayer (it is discussed in more detail in the last chapter).

Many Christians have found this to be a huge advantage in their personal devotions when they struggled to pray; they could use what they had read with inspiration toward God. They have been encouraged in this, using this more effectively than others who are far more skilled, more eloquent, and more to say. I have to agree with what Bishop Wilkins says, "That it is not always necessary here that a person should still keep on in a continued frame of speech; but in private devotions, they may take greater freedom both for his phrase and content. They can sometimes be at a standstill and make a pause; there may be intermissions and blank spaces, in which by meditation they can recover new content to continue in this duty."

Rule 6: If you find your heart so dry that you have nothing to say in prayer, no divine content comes into your thoughts, go humbly before God and tell him that you can say nothing to him, that you can do nothing but groan and cry before him. Go and tell him that without his Spirit you cannot say anything, that without his grace you cannot carry on. Tell him humbly that there will be no morning or evening sacrifice if he does not send down fire from heaven on the altar.

Beg with him for his Spirit, even if it is in sighs and tears. Beg him not to leave your heart so hard or so empty of spiritual things, that he would always supply you with content to communicate with him. God knows the mind of his own Spirit, and he hears those groanings that cannot be uttered, and he understands their language when the heart is imprisoned that it cannot open its mouth. Our heavenly Father hears the groans of the prisoner (Psalm 102:20). There will be a wonderful time of communion with God before you are done, if all you begin with is, "Lord, I cannot pray."

Notice that when your spirit is so heavy and dry, devotion is cold and distracted, and your mind is reluctant, you need to come with humility and surrender before God, especially when you sense that it is because of your own negligence or some guilt your conscience has reminded you of. We should beg forgiveness; and as Bishop Wilkins says, "What we lack in the degrees of our duty, we should be sure to make up in humility; and this will be the most proper use of our failings when we can strengthen ourselves by our very infirmities."

Suggestions About the Content of Prayers

Suggestion 1: It is not necessary to have all the parts of prayer every time you talk to God, though in serious prayers there are only a few that could be left out. What we omit at one time, we can pursue at another so that we fulfill all our duties at the throne of grace.

Let us insist on those things that are burning in our own hearts, especially in secret. This is good advice even for public prayers when those things that deeply affect us concern the people around us. Also, give the parts of prayer enough time and preference, according to our spirit; whether it is praise, request, confession, or thanksgiving. This will not only give us enough to pray about but will keep us passionate and is the best way to affect those that join with us. The things that our fellow worshippers are not concerned with are better put off until we speak to God alone.

Suggestion 2: Let the subject of your prayer suit the occasion and time, place and people with, and for whom, you pray. This will be another source of material and will direct you to proper thoughts and language for every part of prayer.

1. The occasion. If it is morning, we can adore God as the shepherd of Israel who does not slumber or sleep. Then we confess our inability to have defended ourselves through the night, useless and dead as we sleep. Then we give thanks to him that he has protected us from the spirits of darkness, given us

rest, and woken us in peace, *"I lay down and slept; I woke again, for the Lord sustained me"* (Psalm 3:5). Then we ask for divine advice in the affairs of the day, and the presence of God with us through all the worries, work, dangers, and duties.

In the evening, we give thanks to God for the mercies that we requested in the morning. We confess the sins and mistakes of the day and humble our hearts before God. We ask for mercy through the night, along with any praise, confession, and dedication, we feel led to bring, *"In peace I will both lie down and sleep; for you alone, O Lord, make me dwell in safety"* (Psalm 4:8).

So, when we pray before or after a meal; on the Lord's Day or any other days of the week; in a time of war or peace; in a time of public or personal rejoicing; on a day of trouble or humiliation, let our prayer be suited to the particular occasion.

1. The place and the people. In our personal prayer time, we can adore God using these words: "Lord God, who sees in secret, who knows the way that I take, you have commanded your children to seek you in private, and you have promised to publicly reward them." Here we should also confess our specific sins that the world does not know about, and pour out our hearts before God in freedom and truth. We tell him all our mistakes, our weaknesses, our joys and sorrows, our hopes, our fears—everything in our hearts, towards him or others. We talk with God

correctly in prayer when we have a holy relationship with him in secret, and in humility, speak with him as our heavenly friend.

When we pray in a family, the content must be suited to the circumstances of the household, in a confession of family sins, requests, and thanksgiving for family mercies; whether those with whom we live are sick or in health; whether they are in distress or peace; whether fixed in their habitations or moving. Our language to God ought to be suited to this variety of conditions.

If we pray among certain Christians, we draw near to God with the same boldness we use in our secret prayers. We can take more freedom among fellow believers whose hearts are aligned with ours. Then when our faith is passionate, we should give thanks to God for Jesus choosing us; for the atonement and righteousness of the Son of God; for the enlightening and sanctifying work of his Spirit in our hearts; for our expectations of eternal glory. By expressing the joys of our faith to God, the Holy Spirit often uses us to increase the faith and joy of others.

In public worship or in family devotions, where Christians and non-Christians are present, when we speak in prayer we should consider the circumstances of the whole congregation or family, and ask for suitable mercies. But I do not think we should be ashamed to express our faith and hope when speaking to God, where there are many who can join us in that holy language, even though there are some who might not agree. Perhaps this might make those who are not born again, ashamed at their state and so grieved that they are convicted and confused because they cannot join in the same language of faith and hope, joy, and gratitude. It is not necessary for every Christian to lift up their heart to God according to every sentence of public prayer, but only to those suited to their own state, and that they are sincere about.

Suggestion 3: Do not pray long or stretch out what you have to say beyond your own spirit.

God isn't more pleased with prayers because they are long, nor are Christians more edified. When we feel our spirits dry and our hearts strained, it is much better to pray more often than to pray long. We can also cry to God the Holy Spirit to help, even in the middle of our prayer, to carry us forward.

But not all people can pray long. God has given many different natural and spiritual talents and gifts to us. It is not always the best Christian with the greatest gifts that can pray long prayers. Long prayers can lead to many difficulties such as these:

1. Sometimes we get caught up in using unnecessary words to fill our speech because we love long prayers. These are unworthy of God's majesty and inappropriate. Sometimes we are forced to wander off from the subject at hand until we recover our thoughts again; this corrupts and blocks true spiritual worship. We should rather take Solomon's advice on this: *"Be not rash with your mouth, nor let your heart be hasty to utter a word before God, for God is in*

heaven and you are on earth. Therefore let your words be few" (Eccles. 5:2).

2. We get caught in repetitions, saying the same things over and over again, which our Savior does not approve of. "*And when you pray, do not heap up empty phrases as the Gentiles do, for they think that they will be heard for their many words*" (Matt. 6:7). Sometimes in the middle of prayer, we repeat the same words because we are so passionate in our spirit, and there are examples of this in Scripture. But for the most part, our repetitions are not evidence of zeal, but the emptiness of our minds and heart.

3. Long prayers can also become tiring for those that join with us, especially when a prayer is filled with many words, is dull, and has no life or variety. When the Spirit comes on people in some extraordinary occasions, they have continued for an hour or two together with prayers full of content and expression; and instead of an effort to keep going, they found it difficult to stop. Their hearts have been near to God, and they have held the attention of those that joined with them and kept their devotion sincere. Those who went before knew this kind of prayer, but there is little of it these days.

4. We can also take up all the time given for prayer, leaving none for anyone else to do so. Or we take up whatever should follow, and people become restless. And when people need to be somewhere at a specific time afterward, this can spoil their time of devotion. Even when Jacob wrestled with the angel, he had to let him go, because it was daybreak (Gen.

32:26). We must not let one duty crowd out another, so we should make a task harder than it is for ourselves or others, but a pleasure and spiritual exercise.
5. Through excessively long prayers without any real spirit or passion, some careless Christians have given too much ammunition to those who mock religion. It has been seen as a ridiculous way to talk to God and the gift and spirit of prayer have been criticized as a result.

But when the Spirit of God draws the heart to continue in prayer, these difficulties will not follow. While I am discouraging young Christians from the habit of long prayers that come from showing off, or from believing that it will please God more to say many words, or from a shallow heart, I do not want you to think that the shortest prayers are always the best.

Our sinful natures always want to put off God in personal or family devotion with a few quick minutes because we are lazy or bored. In this way, we cut out many of the necessary parts of prayer in confessions, requests, asking for mercy, or thanksgiving.

I also do not think that public prayer should be so short, as though its only purpose was an introduction before the sermon or a blessing after it. Social prayer is a significant part of public worship and we should continue in it long enough to cover the most important purposes of a social address to the throne of grace. Christian wisdom will teach us to determine the length of our prayers according to the occasion and circumstances, and according to the measure of our own ability.

The Method of Prayer

Method is necessary to guide our thoughts, regulate our expressions, arrange the parts of prayer in an order that is understood by those who join us, and inspire and maintain our own devotion and theirs. The same structure is not as necessary as in preaching, but an ordered prayer is acceptable to men, honorable in the world's eyes, and pleasing to God. The Spirit, when he is poured out as a spirit of prayer, does not contradict the rules of a natural and reasonable method, although his methods may have more variety in them.

Some method must be to protect us from confusion so that our thoughts are not chaotic or muddled together. When each part is arranged in its proper place, it prevents repetition and guards against deviations. We can judge what subject naturally follows so that there's no need to fill any empty spaces with content that does not suit the purpose. People who say they pray without any method at all, if they are acceptable and effective in their gift, must be using a secret and a natural method to properly connect one thing with another, even though they have not laid down any rule themselves or taken notice of the order of their own prayers.

The general rules of method in prayer, which I recommend to you, are these three:

Rule 1: Let the general and the specific subjects in prayer be well distinguished, with the generalities being mentioned first and the specifics following them.

For example, in praise, we acknowledge that God is glorious in his nature, self-sufficient, and all-sufficient, and we mention this with reverence and humility; and then we praise him for his power, wisdom, goodness, etc. So, in confession we first acknowledge ourselves as sinners, corrupt by nature, as sinful as the rest of mankind; and then we confess our specific iniquities and our guilt. In our requests we pray first for the global church and the gospel throughout the earth; and then we petition for the churches in our country, city, or the one we belong to.

Sometimes there is a beauty in summing up all the specifics in one generality when we have praised God to the best of our ability, and we cry out, "Lord, you are exalted above all our praises; you are altogether great and glorious." Or when we have confessed several particular sins, we fall down before God filthy and guilty. When we have asked for particular mercies, we then ask that God, who is able to do for us above what we can ask or think, would give all the comforts and blessings that he knows we need. But still, this rule must be observed, that general and specific points must be distinguished enough so that our method of prayer is natural and acceptable.

Rule 2: Let things of the same kind be put together in prayer.

We should not jump from one part to another and then return to the same part again, going backward and forward in confusion. This does not help the mind of the person praying, irritates fellow Christians, and ruins their devotion. This will only lead to useless repetitions, and we shall lose our way.

I will make this exception: sometimes the same matter may come naturally under two or three parts of prayer and be properly mentioned in two or three places. We may mention some of the attributes of God under praise, where we adore him for his perfection, and again when pleading for mercy, when we use his power, wisdom, or goodness as an argument to enforce our requests. We may also mention his attributes in thanksgiving when we bless him for the benefits that come from his goodness, power, and wisdom. So, at the beginning of a prayer, in calling on God, we put in a sentence or two of confession of our unworthiness and a request for divine assistance; and towards the conclusion, we can use a sentence or two consisting of something that will leave a good impression on our minds, even though we may have been mentioned it before.

For example, we may ask forgiveness for all our imperfections; ask that God would hear all our requests in the name of Jesus; recommend our prayers into the hands of our Redeemer, our great High Priest; and commit ourselves to his grace, until we are brought safely to glory. But all this must be done with a variety of words and proper connections, that it will be acceptable, and focus the minds of those with us, that they will be encouraged rather than blocked in prayer.

Rule 3: In every part of prayer, let those things that are objects of our judgment be first mentioned, followed by those that influence and move our emotions.

I don' mean we should follow a manner of prayer like preaching, as some have done, speaking truth without the form of prayer. That is an inappropriate habit some people have followed; when truth is mentioned in prayer, it becomes long and doctrinal. Yet there is a place for divine truths, laying a good foundation for honest words to follow, "Lord, you are good, and you do good; why should I continue so long without tasting your goodness? My sins and iniquities are great, I mourn for them before you in secret! I pour out my heart before you in sorrow because of the many offenses!" Let the language of emotion follow the language of our judgment, for this is the most rational and natural method.

Having laid down these general rules, the best method is to divide the parts of prayer as mentioned in the previous chapter. I do not know of a more natural order of things than this. To begin by calling on God, then to proceed to praise the God we call because of his glory, we are then naturally led to confession, considering what wicked people we are in the presence of God, and to humbling ourselves because of our many sins and needs. When we have given praise to a God of holiness and have brought our needs before him, requests for mercy naturally follow, and these should be accompanied by pleading with arguments as the Spirit and the Bible put into our mouths. Lastly, we surrender ourselves into the hands of God and express our dedication to him. Then we recall the mercies we have received, and out of gratitude give him honor and thanks. And, as he is glorious in himself, and glorious in his works of power and grace, so we bless him and ascribe everlasting glory to him.

It is very useful for beginners in prayer to remember all these points in their order and to express their thoughts and desires before God in this method, from one part to another. Just as it is useful to help and teach us to pray in public, it can also help in our personal devotions.

But remember, we do not have to restrict ourselves to a structure in prayer. Sometimes the mind is so spiritually full of one part of prayer, like thanksgiving or declaration, that words of gratitude and of devoting ourselves to God come first: "Lord, I come to devote myself to you in an everlasting covenant; I am yours through your grace, and through your grace, I will be yours forever," or "Blessed be your name, Lord Almighty, for your abundant blessings that fill my soul; for you have pardoned all my iniquities and healed all my diseases."

Sometimes, even at the beginning of a prayer, when we are insisting on one of the first parts, we receive a divine hint from the Spirit that carries our thoughts and hearts away into another part that is very different and usually comes near the conclusion. And when the Spirit leads us like this, we mustn't quench him in order to tie ourselves to any rules of a prescribed method.

It is not necessary that those who are skilled, talk a lot with God, and have attained this gift of prayer through practice, should bind themselves to only one method of prayer. We can find the prayers recorded in the Bible vary in their order and manner, as the Spirit of God and the hearts of those believers led and guided them. But there is still some method observed.

I am convinced that if young Christians avoid a loose and careless habit of saying whatever comes first to them in prayer, but tried to learn this skill of remembering the parts of prayer and expressing their thoughts in this method, many people in church would realize the gift of prayer and be capable of finding freedom in their hearts, without breaking the rules of a logical and natural method—and this would edify their church and families.

Expression in Prayer

Prayer is a work of the heart; yet in personal and public prayer, the words of the mouth are an incredible advantage.

A person may pray passionately and effectively but use no words. Sometimes the desires of the heart are too big to be expressed when the Spirit is with us working and assisting us to plead with sighs and groans that cannot be uttered (Rom. 8:26). People that are unable to speak can think about their needs and raise their hearts to God in desire for grace. It is not necessary to use language with God because he knows the desires of our hearts and our most secret thoughts. He hears without ears and understands us without our words. But just as language is necessary for public prayer so that others can join in, so we also find it necessary in secret, because there are few people so steady and fixed in their meditation that they can talk with God without ever using words.

Expressions are not just useful to reveal our thoughts, but sometimes to form and perfect the ideas and wishes of our minds. Using words makes us extra conscious of the things we conceive. They serve to awaken the holy passions of the heart as well as to express them. Our expressions sometimes follow and reveal the stirrings of the heart, and sometimes they are dictated by our logic which can motivate the heart and holy emotions. They can fix and engage our senses in worship, regulate as well as increase our devotion. We are told *"Take with you words and return to the Lord; say to him, 'Take away all iniquity; accept what is good'"* (Hos. 14:2). And in the Psalms, we often read about David in personal, secret prayers crying to the Lord with his voice and pleading with his tongue.

Suggestions on Having Rich Expression in Prayer

I will first give suggestions and then some rules about the choice and use of words and expressions.

Suggestion 1: Besides the relationship with God and with ourselves that we heard of in a previous section, strive for the fresh and active sense of the greatness and grace of God, and of your own needs, sins and mercies, whenever you come to pray.

This will give you many good expressions. The passions of the mind, when motivated, help the tongue a lot. They fill the mouth with arguments. They give a natural eloquence to those who do not know the rules of speaking. And they can even compel the dumb to speak. There is an incredible example of this in history, when the son of Croesus the king, Atys, who was mute since childhood, saw his father about to be killed, broke the bonds that tied his tongue, and cried out to save him. Beggars that feel hunger and cold find many ways to express their needs and to plead for relief. Let our spiritual senses be awake and alert and our emotions sensitive, and let them lead; then words will follow.

Suggestion 2: Store up expressions, those you read in the Bible, and have found in other books of devotion or have heard fellow Christians use that have encouraged your heart.

Those that have influenced and touched us at one time do the same at other times—as long as we do not restrict ourselves to them, otherwise, we will become formal and thoughtless in prayer.

While limiting ourselves to a set form of words is not good, sincere, holy, and well-written patterns of prayer can be useful to form our expressions and give us the correct language to pray in. I wish some people were not so quick to throw every single written form out, just as much as those who love them do not idolize each one. But I suppose no one will disagree with using some heartfelt sentences from the Psalms, the complaints of Job, and other holy men when they pray.

These could be called words that the Holy Spirit teaches, and whenever they suit our circumstances, they will always be pleasing to God. The Spirit in praying and preaching will often bless the use of his own language. I am convinced this is one way that he helps our weaknesses and becomes a Spirit of supplication in us, by suggesting specific passages of Scripture that are useful for content and expression in prayer.

One of the best judges of thought and language guarantees us of the beauty and glory of the Bible, and that it can teach us how to pray. This paragraph comes from the Spectator, June 14, 1712. It says: "It happens that the Hebrew idioms run into the English tongue with a grace and beauty: our language has received many elegancies and improvements from that infusion of Hebraisms that come from the poetical passages of the Scriptures; they give a force and energy to our expressions, warm and animate our language, and convey our thoughts in more ardent and intent phrases than any in our own tongue; there is something so passionate in this kind of writing that it often sets the mind alight and makes our hearts burn within us. How cold and dead is a prayer that is composed in the most elegant and polite forms of speech in our natural tongue when it is not emphasized by that sincerity of phrase drawn from the sacred writings? It has been said that if the gods were to talk with men, they would certainly speak in Plato's style; but I think we may say, that when humans converse with their creator, they cannot do it as properly as that of the Holy Scriptures."

To improve in the gift of prayer, we should observe those expressions in our daily reading of the Bible that are suited to the parts of prayer—praise, confession, request, or thanksgiving—and let them be used when we speak to God that day. If we remembered just one verse every day, fixed it in our hearts by frequent meditation, and worked it into our prayers morning and evening, it would become a treasure of spiritual meaning and language, that we can use to address our Maker.

People with no education or social status have achieved this holy skill of prayer simply by having their minds filled with words of Scripture, and have been able to pour out their hearts before God in proper thoughts and language, better than those that have enjoyed the advantage of decent schooling.

However, I would have two warnings about using Scriptural language:

1. We shouldn't paraphrase the words of Scripture too much, or use them in a way that is different from their true meaning. Not that I condemn all paraphrases as there are some used sensibly and acceptably. But if we want to show off our creativity by rephrasing verses where they are different from their original meaning, we will be in danger of misinterpreting the Bible and mistaking the true sense by using it in our prayers this way.
2. We must not use those expressions which are hard to understand or seem ambiguous. If we use such unclear sentences when speaking to God, we might as well pray in an unknown language, which is criticized by Paul (1 Cor. 14:9,14). Do not let the sound of any Hebrew names or obscure verses find their way into our public prayer, even though we might know their meaning, otherwise, we will confuse other Christians.

Suggestion 3: Always be ready to engage in spiritual debate and holy discussions.

This will teach us to speak about the things of God. It is a good habit to remember and talk with each other about the sermons you have heard, the books and verses you have been reading, and especially your own spiritual experience. By this, you will gain a large treasure of language to express your thoughts and emotions.

It is a good practice after you have heard a sermon, to talk with another Christian who also heard it, and go over all the specifics of it so that you can remember it. Then go away and pray over them again; make them the content and substance of your prayer to God. Plead with him to instruct you in the truths that were spoken of; to lead you to perform the deeds recommended and to mourn over the sins that were rebuked; to teach you to trust and live on the promises and comforts proposed, and to wait and hope for the glories revealed in that sermon. Do this often in the same week, if the sermon is suited to your circumstances and condition of your heart. This will give you rich content and expression for prayer.

The reason we lack expressions in prayer is because many times we are not used to speaking about the things of Christianity. Someone with limited skills and no eloquence learns to talk well about the things of his work and business in the world, and hardly ever lacks words to discuss things with his customers. It is because his heart and his tongue are engaged in them all the time. If we become accustomed to speaking frequently about Christian aspects to others, we shall learn to express ourselves much better about the same things when we come before God.

Suggestion 4: Pray sincerely for the gift of speaking well, and ask for the blessing of the Spirit to gain expressions for prayer.

Paul often prayed for the freedom of speech in his ministry, that he may speak the mystery of Christ and reveal it to others (Col. 4:3, 4). So the gift of speaking in prayer is a good request to be made to God, for the advantage of our own hearts and those that join us. The wise man tells us that *"The plans of the heart belong to man, but the answer of the tongue is from the Lord"* (Prov. 16:1). Let us pray that when God has prepared our heart for his worship, he would also teach our tongue to answer the thoughts and desires of the heart and to express them in suitable words to all our spiritual feelings. A variety of holy expressions in prayer is a good and perfect gift that comes from God, the Father of lights and knowledge (James 1:17).

Rules for Using Rich Expression in Prayer

The rules about the choice and use of expressions in prayer are these:

Rule 1: Choose those expressions that best suit your meaning, answer the ideas of your mind, and are fitted to your sense of things.

The design of prayer is to tell God the inner thoughts of your heart. If you speak what is not in the heart, even though the words are excellent, it is just a mockery of God. Let your tongues be the interpreters of your minds. When our hearts are filled with the realization of the attributes or works of God, when our hearts are overpowered with a sense of guilt and unworthiness, or there is an important request, then it is a pleasure to use an expression that speaks our very soul and fulfills all our meaning! And what a pleasure it conveys to all who are with us in the spirit! It helps to motivate them with the same devotion as the words we speak. The royal preacher look for, and took time to find acceptable words in his sermons, that they might be like nails fastened by the master-builder (Eccles. 12:10-11); that is, that they might leave a strong and lasting impression on those who hear, that by piercing deep into the heart, they might be fixed as nails. It is the same reason for choosing the correct words in prayer.

Rule 2: Use a way of speaking that is natural, easy to understand, and acceptable to those with you.

Paul gives directs the Corinthians about this; *"So with yourselves, if with your tongue you utter speech that is not intelligible, how will anyone know what is said? For you will be speaking into the air"* (1 Cor. 14:9). Avoid all foreign and unfamiliar words, or which are old and out-of-date.

Avoid those expressions which are too philosophical, and those which have too much mystical meaning. Avoid a long train of unclear metaphors, or of expressions that are used by cults or factions. Avoid long and obscure sentences, placing your words incorrectly, and do not put in too many parentheses which cloud and confuse the meaning.

There are one or two examples of these improper methods of speaking; not that I have heard these actual phrases used by any Christians in prayer. But as bad habits, the best cure or prevention is seeing them in the clearest and most awful colors, so the errors of expression are best avoided by representing them in their own complete deformity.

This will make us wary and deter us from going near these kinds of mistakes. Without examples of each of these faults, I do not know how else to make Christians understand what should be avoided.

By unfamiliar words, I mean those that are either too old or too new for daily use. Some of these words are still in certain translations of the Bible; many you will find in the old translation of the Psalms in the Book of Common Prayer. They were good for when they were written but are not used anymore. New words are often borrowed from foreign languages, and should not be used in public prayer until they have become so common that there is no difficulty to anyone listening to or speaking them.

By philosophical expressions, I mean those taught in academic institutions to give educated people a shorter and more comprehensive view of things or to distinguish easily between ideas that can be mistaken without this distinction. For example, it is not right to say to God in public prayer, "You are hypostatically three, and essentially one. By the plenitude of perfection in your essence, you are self-sufficient for your own existence and beatitude; who in an incomplex manner eminently, though not formally, includes all the infinite variety of complex ideas that are found among the creatures." This language can be used by someone on their own, accustomed to thinking and meditating in this ways, but other Christians would not be edified by them.

In the language of mystical divinity, there are all sorts of phrases that sects have used, and some have copied, such as "the deiform fund of the soul", the "superessential life," of "singing a hymn of silence"; that God is "an abyss of light," a "circle whose center is everywhere, and his circumference nowhere"; that hell is "the dark world made up of spiritual sulfur and other ingredients not united or harmonized, and without that pure balsamical oil that flows from the heart of God." These are words of vanity that captivate silly people by sounding good but not making sense.

By running long metaphors, I mean using similes or metaphors and going so far as to be doctrinally incorrect. This kind of language is like that of a foolish writer, who says we should "give our hearts to the Lord, cut them with the knife of contrition, take out the blood of your sins by confession, afterward wash it with satisfaction," etc.

By expressions that lean toward denominations, I mean those that would be useless, or even offensive, to Christians of different organizations that join with us in prayer. We shouldn't insist on the differences of doctrine and worship in any church, for example, of infant baptism, when Baptists are praying with us. Our prayers should not have any anger and division, because we must lift up holy hands without wrath (1 Tim. 2:8).

I recommend expressions that are easy to understand, avoiding long and entangled sentences, placing your thoughts and words in an order that those listening may be able to receive and join in. As in all our conversations, debates, and discussions, we should do our best to make everything we say easy to understand, especially in prayer, where the emotions are stirred. This cannot be done if those listening struggle to understand the meaning of what is said.

Rule 3: Let your language be serious and decent, somewhere between grandeur and timidity.

Let it be plain, but not impolite. Let it be clean, but not grand and imposing. Job speaks of choosing his words to reason with God (Job 9:14). Some words are excellent and beautiful; others are rude and disagreeable. Be careful of rough, irregular, and vain expressions that are not suitable for prayer. Use language you would normally generally use in your serious discussions about Christianity when you speak with one another about the things of God. Then the mind will not wander, and the tongue should answer and interpret the mind. The language of a Christian in prayer should clothe his thoughts and dress the heart, and it should be decent and neat, but not arrogant or showy; simple and plain, but not careless, unclean, or rude.

So, avoid fancy language and pretentious style. When you address God in worship, it is a mistake to borrow phrases from secular entertainment and poets—many of their expressions are too light, wild, and airy for such an awesome duty. Too much elegance and fine style in prayer reveals the same pride and vanity of mind like someone wearing too many jewels and fine clothes in the house of God. Our hearts are betrayed as we try our best to make the nicest speech and say the finest things, instead of sincere devotion and praying in the Spirit. If we want to use elevated phrases, Scripture has many of them, and these are acceptable to God and his people.

Avoid low, coarse, and colloquial expressions that may bring about ridiculous ideas, irreverent thoughts, or impure images, in the mind; for these are not good for devotion. It is very irresponsible to speak to God in the same rude and inappropriate manner that others would find unsuitable. God still hears the language of the meanest soul in secret, even though that person cannot express themselves decently. We should equip ourselves with proper methods of expression so that they may be pleasing to those with us.

We do not need to be rough and careless in order to be honest. Sometimes people have been guilty of bringing Christianity and the name of Jesus into disrepute by their irreverent freedom when they speak to God. I do not approve of phrases like "rolling on Christ," "swimming on Christ to dry land," or "taking a lease of Christ for all eternity," or "hanging with Jesus."

I think we can fulfill the command of coming boldly to the throne of grace without such language. People who borrow similes search all the drains of nastiness to find metaphors for their sins and in praying for the coming of Christ, they "fold up the heavens like an old cloak," and "shovel days out of the way." Remember that words, as well as things, grow old and annoying. Some expressions, that might have appeared proper sixty years ago would be highly offensive to the ears of today. It is not a good enough apology for these phrases, that men of great education and sincerity use them.

Rule 4: Look for expressions that show your passion and carry life and spirit with them; that can motivate and stir our love, hope, joy, sorrow, fear, and faith, as well as express those characteristics.

This is the way to raise, assist, and maintain devotion. We should avoid the style that looks more like preaching, which some people with long prayers are guilty of. They speak to the people and teach them the doctrines of Christianity and the mind and will of God, rather than telling God the desires of their own minds. They have wandered away from God to preach to men. This is contrary to the nature of prayer, because prayer is our own address to God, declaring our sense of spiritual things and pouring out our hearts before him.

There are several modes of expression that will help:

1. Exclamations, that show an affectionate wonder, a sudden surprise, or violent impression of anything on the mind.

   - *"Oh, how abundant is your goodness, which you have stored up for those who fear you"* (Psalm 31:19).
   - *"How precious to me are your thoughts, O God! How vast is the sum of them!"* (Psalm 139:17).
   - *"Wretched man that I am! Who will deliver me?"* (Rom. 7:24).

1. Interrogations, when anything we declare from God is turned into a question to make it more emphatic.

- *"Where shall I go from your Spirit? Or where shall I flee from your presence?"* (Psalm 139:7).
- *"Do I not hate those who hate you, O Lord?"* (Psalm 139:21).
- *"Who will deliver me from this body of death?"* (Rom. 7:24).

1. Appeals to God, concerning our own needs or sorrows, our sincere and deep sense of the things we speak to him.

- *"Lord, you know everything; you know that I love you"* (John 21:17).
- So David appeals to God, "The wrongs I have done are not hidden from you" (Psalm 69:5).
- *"You have kept count of my tossings; put my tears in your bottle"* (Psalm 56:8).
- *"You know that I am not guilty...my witness is in heaven, and he who testifies for me is on high"* (Job 10:7; 16:19).

1. Challenges are a kind of interrogation, not only used to express deep disappointment but to enforce any argument in pleading with God for mercy for his people or the destruction of his enemies.

- *"Look down from heaven and see, from your holy and beautiful habitation. Where are your zeal and your might? The stirring of your inner parts and your compassion are held back from me...O Lord, why do you make us wander from your ways and harden our heart, so that we fear you not?"* (Isaiah 63:15,17).

- *"Awake, awake, put on strength, O arm of the Lord; awake, as in days of old, the generations of long ago. Was it not you who cut Rahab in pieces, who pierced the dragon? Was it not you who dried up the sea, the waters of the great deep?"* (Isaiah 51:9-10).
- *"Will the Lord spurn forever, and never again be favorable?"* (Psalm 77:7).
- *"O Lord God of hosts, how long will you be angry?"* (Psalm 80:4).
- *"Why do you hide your face? Why do you forget our affliction and oppression?"* (Psalm 44:24).
- God invites his people thus to argue with him, *"Come now, let us reason together, says the Lord"* (Isaiah 1:18).

And holy men in humble and reverent challenges have pleaded their case before God, and their words are recorded as our patterns.

1. Options, or wishes, that show serious and sincere desires.

- *"Oh, that I might have my request"* (Job 6:8).
- *"Oh that my ways may be steadfast in keeping your statutes!"* (Psalm 119:5).

1. Apostrophes; in the middle of our prayer we suddenly turn away from what we were saying, and turn to our hearts, being led by an intense spiritual thought.

- *"Preserve me, O God, for in you I take refuge. I say to the Lord, 'You are my Lord; I have no good apart from you'"* (Psalm 16:1-2).

In meditations, psalms, hymns, or other devotional compositions, these apostrophes may be longer and more frequent, but in prayer, they should be very short, except when the speech is turned from one person of the Trinity to another: "Great God, have you not promised that your Son should have the lost for his inheritance and that he should rule the nations? Jesus, how long before you assume this kingdom? When will you send your Spirit to enlighten and convert the world? When, Holy Spirit, will you come and shine your light and grace through all the earth?"

1. Inseminations, or emphasizing our expressions, which show an enthusiastic and passionate emotion.

- "O Lord, God of vengeance, O God of vengeance, shine forth!" (Psalm 94:1).
- *"My soul waits for the Lord more than watchmen for the morning, more than watchmen for the morning"* (Psalm 130:6).
- "Blessed be his glorious name forever; may the whole earth be filled with his glory! Amen and Amen!" (Psalm 72:19).

But let us be careful to distinguish between those repetitions that arise from a real passion of spirit and those that are just used to lengthen a prayer or that come from a dry heart and lack of content. It is much better in public prayer, to stay in our present state and shorten the prayer than to fill our time with many repetitions, such as, "Lord our God if it is your will; we ask you; we beg you; Lord, have mercy on us." For though some of these expressions can be repeated several times in a prayer, filling up every empty space and stretching out every sentence with them is not acceptable to others with us, nor does it help our devotion or theirs.

Rule 5: Do not always just use one form of words to express your request, or try and avoid an expression because you used it before.

The exact uniformity of words or trying to use lots of different expressions in every prayer is not always healthy. It is best to stick between these two extremes. We should rather try to be equipped with a rich variety of holy language so that our prayers can always have something new and something engaging in them, and not tie ourselves to always express something in the same words, because this can become formal and dull.

But, if we are guilty of always using new words which we never used before, we will sometimes miss the best and most spiritual meaning, and end in error. These prayers will look like a creative invention, and efforts of the head, more than the breathings of the heart. Copying those Christians and ministers that are skilled in prayer will be the best in most of these cases.

The Voice in Prayer

Wonderful expressions and a beautiful voice do not make our worship more acceptable to God; yet because we are flesh and spirit, it does help if there is harmony in the voice of the person speaking. The content, method, and expressions may be well chosen in prayer, but it is possible for the voice to spoil it for everyone else. When well-written speeches are recited in a cold, harsh, or ungrateful way, the beauty is lost.

Some people have a very sweet and tuneful voice, and whatever they speak is pleasing. Others must make more effort and follow rules and suggestions so that their pronunciation is correct. Because we are prone to drift off lose attention despite all the best attempts, it is necessary to recognize and avoid bad pronunciation that could put others off.

In personal prayer, there is no need for a voice because God hears a whisper as well as a sigh and a groan. Yet some Christians cannot pray by themselves without using their voice to some degree. It is also not a bad thing to have a convenient place for this personal time, because you can express your emotions more, and also, if you focus on your voice, practice speaking better for when you are in public.

The general rule I have for managing the voice in prayer is this: let us use the same voice we usually speak in during a serious conversation, especially on intense subjects. This is the best advice to regulate the sound and the words. Our own voice is the most natural choice, rather than using a different one in prayer, which will only cause others to think we are hypocrites.

The suggestions are these:

Suggestion 1: Let your words be pronounced clearly and not be shortened by cutting out vowels or syllables, affected groanings, or useless sounds, coughing, etc., which some, have been guilty of.

If you cut off and lose the last syllable of your word, or mumble the last words of the sentence and drop your voice so that others cannot hear, they will think it is because you didn't speak properly or are afraid to be heard.

However, if you lengthen your sentences with strange sounds, the prayer time could end up becoming a joke. What sounds like clearing your throat or emphasizing other sounds, others might think you are doing to try to prolong your sentences, stretch your prayers, and recover your thoughts of what to say next. Therefore, when you become passionate about what you are saying, or when you think about what you will say next, it is better to make a long pause and keep silent than to start making irrelevant sounds.

Suggestion 2: Let every sentence be spoken loudly enough to be heard, but not so loud that they frighten or offend.

Between these two extremes, there are many volumes that can convey our emotions and the different parts of our prayer. At the beginning of prayer, a lower voice is better as it shows humility and reverence when we enter into the presence of God. It is also good for the throat not to get too loud too quickly because it is harder to become quiet again afterward. Some people start their prayers off so loudly that they startle everyone; others begin so low that it sounds like a personal prayer that all those present shouldn't be part of. Both these extremes are to be avoided.

Suggestion 3: Find an average between rapid and sluggish speech, because both are not good.

If you are too quick, your words will be rushed; they will run on to each other and become a confusion. It is necessary to have measured gaps between your words, and larger ones between your sentences so that everything can be pronounced distinctly and clearly.

Pauses and stops will give others time to understand and reflect on what you say, and to join with you; it will allow you to breathe, making it easier and more pleasant for yourselves. Also, when people rush into a non-stop flow of words without rests or pauses, they are in danger of saying things they do not mean before God, letting their tongue run faster than their thoughts as well as the thoughts of those with them. Some people begin a sentence in prayer and then have to break off and start again, or if they carry on, it is so inconsistent that it makes little sense or is grammatically bad. This has allowed others to mock prayer and has been dishonorable to God.

It all comes from a rush of the tongue into the middle of a sentence before the mind has made complete sense of it.

On the other hand, if you are too slow, this will become boring for others to listen to. They will listen, and then have to wait for the next sentence to stimulate their own thoughts so that they can continue with you. This will make our prayers heavy and dull. However, a mistake like this is better than rushing through your sentences, and its consequences are less damaging.

In general, let the meaning of each sentence be a rule to guide your voice, whether it must be loud or soft, quick or slow. In calling on God, humble praise, confession of sin, and declaration, a slower and a more modest voice is best, as well as in every other part of prayer where nothing too emotional is expressed. But in requests, pleadings, thanksgiving, and rejoicing in God, enthusiasm, joy, and victory will lift the voice higher, and passion will naturally make our language faster.

Suggestion 4: Let proper expression be used, according to the meaning of what is said.

There are so many rules about proper expression, but logic and instinct will show us what is correct if we listen. However, to keep us from making mistakes, here are a few things to avoid:

1. Avoid a monotonous voice, when every word and sentence is spoken without any difference in sound, like pupils repeating their lessons in one dull note, which shows they do not understand the sense and value of the author. Even though people who speak like this might be sincere and true, such pronunciation will be seen as careless and thoughtless, as though they were unconcerned about what they were doing and have no feelings about it.
2. Avoid putting accents on words incorrectly and wrong pronunciation. Although the sentences are different in meaning, length, or expression, the voice follows the same patterns. For example, beginning every sentence in prayer with a high voice and ending

it in a low one; or starting each line with deep bass and finishing it with a high-pitched, sharp sound. This is as if a musician has only one tune or a single set of notes and repeats it in every line of a song, which would not sound graceful.

Another instance of false pronunciation is when strong accents are put on little words and particles that have little meaning in the sentence. Some people put emphasis on words like 'they,' 'that,' 'of,' and 'by,' while the phrases and expressions that should be highlighted are said with no emotion or priority.

Another example is when a plain sentence that deserves no passion or enthusiasm, is said with lots of force and power; or when the most fervent and emotional expressions are spoken calmly, with a composed voice. All of these are unnatural and should be avoided by anyone who wants to speak properly, to edify others in the meeting.

The last instance is when our voice becomes musical, as though we were singing instead of praying. Some sincere Christians fall into the trap of enjoying the sound of their voice in personal devotions, and with no one to tell them how irritating it is to others, it has become a habit.

1. Avoid coloring every word and sentence to extremes, as if you were on a stage. Some people have made this mistake because no one has warned them against it and because it appears as though they are showing off, it leads to criticism.

One example is to say every humble and mournful sentence as though they were actually crying. Critics have called it whining, and have blamed the church for putting on an act because of a few people doing this.

Another instance is when we express every good sentence, promise or comfort, joy or hope, in such a free and airy manner, with too much happiness, or with a wide smile. It looks a bit too easy and friendly when dealing with a God who is so great. Every strange and unpleasant tone shouldn't be allowed, nor should we come before God in humility on our knees but speak proudly and magnificently, otherwise our voice will contradict our actions. This could look like irreverence and irritate those who hear us.

Gestures in Prayer

It might not be thought of as a part of the gift, but because it is so much a part of the outward display of prayer, I will include it here.

Since we are commanded to pray always and at all times, there can be no specific posture of the body for short prayers and whispers to God: while we lie in our beds, sit at our tables, or are exercising, our hearts can reach our heavenly Father and have a sweet conversation with him. We can see this in the verse about David, where it says, *"Then King David went in and sat before the Lord and said, 'Who am I, O Lord God, and what is my house, that you have brought me thus far?'"* (1 Chron. 17:16). But when we draw near to God in special times of prayer, there should be a greater degree of seriousness. In everything that relates to it, we must compose ourselves with reverence so that we can worship God with our bodies as well as with our spirits (1 Cor. 6:20).

Let us first consider the posture of the whole body, and then look at the specific parts of it.

1. The postures that the Bible and logic tell us are proper for prayer are standing, kneeling, or prostration.

Prostration is sometimes used in personal prayer, when we are filled with a sense of sin and fall flat on our face before God and pour out our heart before him, where these thoughts and the work of grace produces unusual expressions of humility and surrender. We find this in the Bible on many occasions: Abraham fell on his face before God (Gen. 17:3), Joshua before Jesus, the captain of the host of God (Josh. 5:14), and Moses, Ezekiel, and Daniel did the same. Also in the New Testament, when John fell at the feet of the angel to worship him, thinking it was Jesus (Rev. 19:10). Who wouldn't fall down to the ground in the presence of God himself?

Kneeling is the most frequent position used and logically leads us into an expression of humility, our needs, for mercy, and in praise and dependence on God. This posture has been practiced in all ages and all nations, even where the light of Scripture has never shined. It is very acceptable for worship in public gatherings, as well as in families or our personal devotions. There are so many examples and suggestions for this posture in the Bible that can prove it: Solomon (2

Chron. 6:13), Ezra (Ezra 9:5), Daniel (Dan. 6:10), Jesus (Luke 22:41), and Paul (Acts 20:36; 21:5 and Eph. 3:14).

Lastly, standing is a position that is good for prayer, especially when the more humble gestures are not convenient. The same way that standing up before someone we respect is a sign of honor that we pay them, so standing before God is acceptable to our reverence of the One we address and worship. There are examples of this gesture in the Bible. Our Savior said to his disciples, *"Whenever you stand praying"* (Mark 11:25); and the tax collector stood to the side and prayed (Luke 18:13). Standing seems to have been the common gesture of prayer in a large public gathering (2 Chron. 20:4-5,13). It is good to join in the same custom of those Christians with whom we worship, whether standing or kneeling since neither of them are singled out in the Bible as the only way.

But sitting, or other postures of rest and laziness, shouldn't be practiced in serious moments of prayer, unless someone is sick or old, or the prayer is so long that it is difficult to stay standing or kneeling. Whatever position keeps the mind focused and fits in with prayer, will be accepted by God. His rule that he has given, which should be remembered, is that bodily exercise profits little; for he looks mainly at the heart, and he requires obedience, not sacrifice.

1. There are other parts of the body that can be used in prayer, and to protect us from mistakes, these positions are listed here:

The head should not have to move much. Many people have been mocked and criticized because they toss and shake their heads or nod excessively while praying. However, in times of humility, hanging the head down is a good method to express a state of mind. It is the same with the tax collector we read about, and the Jews in the time of Ezra, who bowed their heads and worshipped the Lord with their faces to the ground (Neh. 8:6). But in our expressions of hope and joy, it is natural to lift up the head while we believe that our redemption is near (Luke 21:28). Paul's advice is that a person who prays should cover his head so as not to bring dishonor to themselves (1 Cor. 11:4).

God has created many different facial gestures that can reveal the state of the mind, especially when moved by emotion.

In prayer, the whole face should be sincere and serious, to express holy awe and reverence of God's majesty and the importance of speaking with him.

In confessing sin, as we express the sorrows of our hearts, sadness will appear in our features. The despair can be seen there and, according to the Bible, shame and confusion will cover our faces. The humble sinner blushes before God at remembering his guilt (Jer. 51:51; Ezra 9:6). Passion in our requests, and joy when we give thanks to God for his mercies, and rejoicing in hope, will be revealed by pleasant expressions in our faces.

But we must be careful to avoid our Savior's rebuke, who rebuked the Pharisees for twisting and deforming their faces for the whole day of fasting and prayer (Matt. 6:16). While we are praying, an appearance of devotion is natural and proper and acceptable to God. But at the same time, it is best that any facial expression linked to our emotions should not be too revealing. The devotion of our hearts should be warmer and stronger than that of our faces. And we should beware of distorting our features, like grimacing and twisting our mouths, eyes, and nose to squeeze out our words or our tears, which can distract and annoy others when they see it. We should also avoid yawning or displaying sleepy gestures, which show a lazy mind. Jeremiah's words are harsh when he says, *"Cursed is he who does the work of the Lord with slackness"* (Jer. 48:10).

Lifting our eyes to heaven is very natural in prayer, and is mentioned often in the Psalms (Psalm 121:1; 123:1; 141:8). But sometimes in despair and concern for sin, it is decent to look down to the ground like the tax collector, as though we are unworthy to lift up our eyes to heaven where God is (Luke 18:13).

Mostly, wandering eyes that take notice of everything should be avoided in prayer. Even though a person that prays can keep focused while looking around (which seems very difficult to do), others around them might judge that our hearts are wandering as much as our eyes are, and will suspect that we are not sincere. Some people like to always keep their eyes closed in prayer so that they are not distracted by what they see and lose the train of their thoughts, and have their hearts led astray by their senses. It is also not totally incorrect to shut our eyes and exclude the world while we are talking with God. But in this and other advice, I would always excuse those with any natural weaknesses, and they must use those methods that make prayer easiest for them.

Lifting hands up, sometimes folded together, or sometimes apart, is a very natural expression of seeking help from God (Psalm 28:2; 134:2). The elevation of the eyes and the hands is the most logical action in addressing God that even non-Christians practice, as we can see in many of their written accounts. We also find it mentioned in the Bible.

And as lifting up of the hands to heaven is a very natural gesture when a person prays for himself, so when an elder or minister prays for a blessing to come onto a person, it is very natural to lay his hand on the head of the person he prays for. We find this practice all through history. It was used by the prophets and apostles when they pronounced authoritative and divine blessings on people and performed miracles. I do not only see it as a prophetic blessing but as a natural expression for a divine blessing from a father to a son, from an older person to a younger, from a minister to other Christians, especially those who are young in Christ. Therefore, when a person is set apart for any position in the church, while prayers are made for a spiritual blessing to come to him, laying on of hands is logical.

Concerning other parts of the body, there is no need for any suggestions or advice. A calm, quiet, and standard posture are decent. Any actions that are noisy are not good, because the prayer becomes distracting. Some people even clap or thump along to the beat and music of their own sentences, which is annoying

In personal devotion, where we can really express our emotions; sighs, groans, and weeping are acceptable, and our body and attitude are moved with the mind. But in public, these should not be acted on, except in extraordinary times when the whole congregation is convinced that they come from the heart. If we get into the habit of using actions or noises made by our hands, feet, or any other parts, it will make others think that our minds are not seriously engaged, or it will look like we are being irreverent.

Family Prayer

Since it is necessary for those who pray to abstain from noisy actions, it is also true for those joining in to not disturb the time with similar gestures and noise. It is not good during family prayer for people to spend lots of time getting onto their knees, adjusting their clothes, moving their chairs, greeting those that pass by, and coming in after the prayer has begun. It is rude to move and get up while the two or three last sentences are being spoken, as though the prayer was so unpleasant and boring that they wished it was over. Often, it is the knee that is the only part that is reverent to God, while all the other parts of the body are lazy, trying to be comfortable, and thoughtless. Some people do not come in until the prayer is started and then fidget and create a disturbance to find their place. To prevent these irregularities, I would persuade the person that prays not to begin until all those who intend to join in the family worship are present, and that even before the chapter is read; because the Bible shouldn't be used in a family other than the ringing of a bell at church, to tell the people that prayer is starting.

Grace Before and After Meals

Another part of social worship in a family is giving thanks before and after meals. We need to look at this since mistakes and improper ways of doing so have crept in.

Some have become used to muttering a few words with a very low voice, as though some secret charm consecrates the food and there is no need for the rest to join in the requests. Others are so loud that it seems as if they want a thousand people to hear them.

Some perform this prayer with a casual, familiar attitude as if they had no sense of the great God that they are speaking to; others put on an unnatural seriousness and change their voice, and even their face so that others laugh and joke about it.

It is also the habit of some to rush through a single sentence or two, and they are finished before anyone else can even lift a thought up to heaven. And some speak a blessing on the church and the king but seem to forget that they are only giving thanks for the food they have received and are asking God to bless it. They go into a long prayer that has nothing to do with the table before them.

The general rules of wisdom, together with observing the customs of the place where we live, can correct all these mistakes and teach us that a few sentences suited to the occasion, spoken normally, are enough, especially if any strangers are present. If we are in mixed company, many times it is best for each person to pray to God by themselves. But in a Christian family, or where everyone is in agreement and the circumstances allow, only a few holy expressions are necessary to give thanks for the food we receive. It is also good to include thanks for any other gift of God at that time.

When a person is eating alone, I do not see the necessity of standing up to bless the food, since this can be done in any position that fits with short prayers. But in the company of others, the custom of standing up is more decent and honorable than sitting down as we give thanks.

We have spoken about the proper gestures for prayer, and I hope they are useful to maintain dignity and to pay honor to God with our bodies and our hearts. We do not have to be like lifeless statues in prayer, but we also do not need to get carried away. The habits and rituals of Christianity are not as many or as detailed as the Jewish rites; nor are they theatrical actions or superstitious sayings like those of the Catholics. We do not need to be masters of ceremonies in order to pray correctly to God, as long as we follow simple manners that logic dictates and follow the commands and examples that the Bible confirms.

Remark: Though the gestures in preaching are very different from those of prayer, most of the rules that are prescribed for the expression and the voice in prayer can be applied to preaching. But the difference is that in preaching the same rules are not always necessary, because we speak to men in the name and authority of God, we have greater freedom of language and gestures. But in prayer, as sinful beings addressing a holy God, everything we do must be composed in humility.

General Suggestions on the Gift of Prayer

In conclusion, I will list these five general suggestions:

Suggestion 1: Stick to the middle of accurately and legalistically keeping all the rules I have given and carelessly ignoring them.

Every rule has its own reason, so it is good to follow it when the right circumstances arise. I have tried to only say what might be useful understanding, attaining, and practicing the gift of prayer. Our many mistakes and forgetfulness, failing to understand, the wanderings of our thoughts, and our shifting emotions, require our best attempts to find the correct way in prayer.

But, I do not want you to stick so closely to all these forms in content, method, expression, voice, and gesture, that you feel you are under obligation and a burden that will deprive your heart of the freedom that the Spirit gives us to be able to pray. When the heart is full of good things to say to the Lord, the tongue will be like the pen of a ready writer (Psalm 45:1). Such focus of thought, such passionate holy emotions, will often produce wonderful fluency and variety of expressions that a person is carried beyond constraints of rules.

Make sure the character of prayer is at work in your heart with power. Let this be your priority; and you will find it natural and easy to pray according to most of the rules I have given, without even trying. For example, a man in a musical mood, without following the rules, can compose some harmonies that are wonderful for everyone that hears him.

Suggestion 2: Observe ministers and fellow Christians who display the most edifying gifts.

In content, method, expression, voice, and gesture, try to imitate those with good reputations for encouraging and maintaining prayer. At the same time, take notice of all the mistakes that others make, in order to avoid them when you pray.

Suggestion 3: Use any proper means to find a good presence of mind and holy courage in prayer.

Though shyness is a natural weakness, it can become sinful if you indulge it, and many gifts have been buried in silence this way. Most people that begin to pray in public, feel shy, and it has different effects on them. Some lose their calm which regulates their expressions and are pushed to finish their prayers like a pupil rushing through their lesson or an alarm that rings until it is stopped. Others hesitate at every sentence, feeling a halt in their speech, and can say no more. Some, whose minds are equipped and prepared, have lost their train of thought and ended in confusion because of shyness.

Courage and confidence are natural talents, but they can also be learned and acquired through the proper means. Here are a few of them:

1. Get over the shame of being a Christian or being called religious, that you won't worry about what the world thinks—when they mock and make fun of godly people.

2. Enjoy and take part in Christian conversation as often as you can. If you are used to speaking to people about the things of God without blushing, you will be able to speak to God in the presence of people with holy confidence.
3. Make an effort to attain this gift of prayer, and practice it often on your own for a while doing so in public.
4. Make sure your heart is always well prepared, and know the content of your prayer beforehand when you make your first public attempts.
5. Try to be in awe of the majesty of God to whom you speak than of the opinions of those humans you are with, that you may forget you are in their company while you address the most high God. When you find your heart becoming shy and sinking away, encourage it and say, "I dare to speak to the almighty God, how can I be afraid of man?"
6. Do not be too sensitive about your own reputation in these things. This softness of spirit is what we call self-consciousness. When we are going to speak in public, this makes the mind weak, causes us to rush, and makes us perform worse than we do in secret. Rather, let us maintain a noble disregard for the criticisms of people and speak with the same courage as though no one but God was present.
7. First try in the company of one or two people, maybe close friends that you know well so that you are not afraid or concerned about their opinions of your performance. Or join with other young Christians

and make times to pray together; this is an excellent way to obtain the gift of prayer.
8. Do not try to say long prayers in your first public attempts, rather be short. Say a few common and necessary requests, then go on to the next parts as far as your gifts and courage increase.
9. Do not be discouraged if your first attempts are not as successful as you hoped. Many Christians have a glorious gift in prayer, even though they started out overwhelmed with shyness and confusion. Do not let Satan succeed in tempting you to throw it all away.
10. Let one of your requests to God be that you may be filled with Christian courage and freedom of speech, as Paul often prayed. He who gives every good and perfect gift will not deny you what is so necessary to be able to pray.

Suggestion 4: Ask a Christian friend to help point out notice any mistakes that you may behave in your prayers, especially when you are learning.

The most valuable friends are those who will go through the trouble of giving you an honest and obliging hint of any errors you are making. It is not possible for us to judge the tone of our own voice or the gestures that we use, and whether they are acceptable to others. Our friends can give a more unbiased judgment than we can.

Without this helpful criticism, some people have developed bad habits when speaking in public and prayer: incorrect tones, improper accents, facial distortions, and various other mistakes, which they carried with them for the rest of their life. These have often opened up worship to ridicule and blocked others that join with them.

Suggestion 5: Practice prayer often, not only in secret but with one another.

Even if every rule was fixed in your memories, without frequent practice you will never grow in skill as a person who prays.

As with our godly characteristics, when we put them into action, they become stronger and shine brighter, give God more glory, and serve others, so it is with every gift of the Holy Spirit; it is developed by frequent exercise.

Therefore, Paul tells the young evangelist Timothy not to neglect to stir up the gift that is in him, even though the gift was given in an extraordinary way, by the laying on of hands (2Tim. 1:6). And that is why some serious Christians who have less knowledge will be better in the gift of prayer than people who are more educated, are cleverer, and have good judgment: because, though they do not understand the rules so well, they practice much more. The general truth is that he who prays most prays best.

Study Guide

Some people are gifted in prayer, some in worship, others in serving, etc. We often find ourselves boxed in by recognizing skills and then only sticking to what we are good at. In this chapter, it is clear that the gift of prayer is more evident in certain people than in others. But Watts admits that rather than be content with the little or much that we have received, we can attain it even more in our lives. His detailed guide on the words, the voice, the times, and the actions we should use can be very helpful in this regard.

It is easy to read, reflect by ourselves, and think that we have understood what something means for our own lives. But Watts saw the importance of discussing things over with trusted friends and elders. "Talking over the things which you have read with your companions fixes them on the mind." Not only does it bring clarity, but can allow others to point out areas in our own lives that we often cannot or will not see.

This study guide is useful as a basis for a group discussion or study. Use the questions to stimulate conversations that can lead to understanding prayer even more, as well as those areas we may struggle with or need help with.

1. What do you understand about the idea that prayer is a gift? Read 1 Peter 4:10 where it says, *"As each has received a gift, use it to serve one another, as good stewards of God's varied grace."* Does this relate to prayer?
2. What is your view on pre-composed prayers versus spontaneous prayers? Which one do you often lean towards when you pray?
3. Why is the content of our prayers so important that a whole portion is spent explaining and directing us to acquire it and use it?
4. Ask your trusted friends if there is anything that may be annoying or incorrect with your
5. Content
6. Method

7. Expressions
8. Voice
9. Gestures
10. What is your view on saying grace at mealtimes? Should they be given as much consideration as our prayers in church?
11. It is important to get the order, content, and delivery of our prayers right, but what about our hearts? Compare Psalm 45:1, Matthew 12:34, and Luke 6:45.
12. What is the difference between the skill of speaking and expressing yourself well and the gift of being able to pray well?

3

THE GRACE OF PRAYER

We shall now look at the internal and spiritual part of prayer, usually called the grace of prayer.

I will explain what it means and show how the term is correctly used. Then I will mention those inner spiritual exercises of the mind required in prayer and give suggestions and advice on how to attain them. It will be a brief overview so that I do not repeat what others have already said about it.

The Difference Between the Grace and the Gift

Grace implies the free and undeserved favor of one person toward another inferior to him. In the New Testament, it is commonly used to signify the favor and mercy of God toward sinful beings, which are free and undeserved. Because our natures are corrupt and opposite to what is good, whenever they are changed and drawn to God and holy things, this is done by God's power working in us. Therefore, this change of nature, this renewed state of mind, is called grace.

These are the differences between integrity, holiness, and grace:

Integrity is the essence of everything good, without actually referring to God. The characters and actions of non-Christians are called virtues or integrity. This word applies to self-control, good morals, generosity, and everything that relates to ourselves and our neighbors, rather than to religion.

Holiness is when all those good characteristics and actions are devoted and performed to God's glory. The word 'holy' means something that is devoted or dedicated.

Grace refers to the same characteristics as a product of God's favor. Sometimes this word is used in a comprehensive sense to mean all the Christian characteristics or the universal habit of holiness.

In this way, we may understand these texts: *"For from his fullness we have all received, grace upon grace"* (John 1:16); and *"But grow in the grace and knowledge of our Lord and Savior Jesus Christ"* (2 Pet. 3:18). And so in our common language when we say that a person is a graceless sinner, or they have no grace at all, we mean they have no good character. And when we say someone is truly gracious or has a principle of grace, we mean they are Christians with integrity.

Sometimes the phrase, 'Grace of Prayer,' is used in the singular, meaning one inclination or holy principle in the mind. So we say, the grace of faith, the grace of repentance, the grace of hope or love. *"But as you excel in everything—in faith, in speech, in knowledge, in all earnestness, and in our love for you—see that you excel in this act of grace also"* (2 Cor. 8:7).

Sometimes it is used in a broader, but not a universal, sense, and implies all those holy qualifications that belong to one action or duty. So we read of the grace that belongs to a conversation, *"Let your speech always be gracious"* (Col. 4:6); the grace of singing, *"singing psalms and hymns and spiritual songs, with thankfulness [grace] in your hearts to God"* (Col. 3:16); and the grace of worship, *"Therefore let us be grateful [and have grace] for receiving a kingdom that cannot be shaken, and thus let us offer to God acceptable worship, with reverence and awe"* (Heb 12:28). And the grace of prayer, *"I will pour out on the house of David and the inhabitants of Jerusalem a spirit of grace and pleas for mercy"* (Zech. 12:10).

In our common understanding, the grace of prayer is not one single act or habit of the mind, but it implies all those holy characteristics which are to be exercised. It consists of being ready to engage in those acts of the sanctified mind, will, and emotions that are suited to prayer.

And that is the great difference between the gift and the grace of prayer. The gift is the outside, the shape of the duty. The grace is the heart and spirit that gives it life, energy, and power, which makes it acceptable to God and effective for us.

The gift consists mainly in being focused and alert in our minds according to the various parts of prayer and expressing those thoughts when speaking to God. The grace consists in the inner workings of the heart and conscience toward God. The gift has a show and appearance of holy desires and affections; but holy emotions, sincere desires, and real communication with God belong only to the grace of prayer.

The gift and the grace are often separated from each other. The gift of prayer can be attained through study, practice, and the work of the Spirit to those who know nothing of true grace. There can also be the grace of prayer in some hearts who have a very small degree of this gift and hardly know how to form their thoughts and desires into a regular method or to express those desires in decent language.

Some people, as it says in Matthew 7, pour out many words before God in prayer, preach like apostles or angels, or cast out demons in Jesus' name, but Jesus does not know them, because they have no grace. On the other hand, some people who are close to God, chatter and cry like a swallow or a crane, as Hezekiah did, but have a passionate habit in the grace of prayer. Where both the gift and the grace meet together in one person, we find a Christian who brings honor to God and has a greater capacity and prospect of doing service for others in the world. They edify and comfort other Christians.

The actions of a sanctified heart in prayer can be called the grace of the Holy Spirit that are exercised. Some of these belong to the work and worship of prayer, and others are specific to the various parts of the duty.

Grace in Prayer

This is the grace that belongs to the whole work or duty of prayer:

1. **Faith or belief in God,** his perfect knowledge, and his gracious notice of everything we say in prayer. This is the rule we are given: *"Whoever would draw near to God must believe that he exists and that he rewards those who seek him"* (Heb. 11:6). We should do our best to remind ourselves of God's existence, though we do not fully know him; of his presence, though he is invisible; and of his justice and mercy towards our actions. We do this so that prayer may not be a ritual or ceremony but performed in the hope of pleasing God and receiving from him. This demonstration of an active faith runs through every part of prayer and gives spirit and power to it.
2. **A seriousness of spirit.** Put aside any trivial, superficial attitudes when coming into the presence of God. When we speak to the Creator, who is also our Judge, about the spiritual concerns, our hearts must be sincere and not casual as if we are discussing ordinary things with our friends. Indecent selfishness should never be allowed when we pray, especially since we are only dust and ashes speaking to an awesome God.
3. **Spirituality should be part of prayer** because we are shifting our attention from earthly things and other people to fix our attention on God and communicate with him who lives in heaven. If our thoughts are full of food and drink, and the business of this life, we will not be seeking the favor and face of God, as devoted Christians should. The things of the world must be put aside for that time and stay at the bottom of the mountain, while we walk up

higher to offer our sacrifices and meet God, as Abraham did.

Our aims and desire should grow more spiritual as we continue in prayer. And though God allows us to talk with him about many of our daily affairs in prayer, let us make sure that the things of our hearts and the eternal world are always a priority. And whatever cares of this life enter into our prayers and are laid out before the Lord, let us see make sure our aims are spiritual, that our very desires of earthly comforts may be purified from all carnal ends and sanctified to some divine purposes, to the glory of God, to the honor of the gospel and to the salvation of souls.

1. **A sincerity of heart** is another grace in prayer, whether we speak to God concerning his own glories, give him thanks for his goodness, confess our sins before him, or express our desire for mercy, let our hearts and our mouths agree, that we are not mocking God, who searches the and tests the heart for any hypocrisy.
2. **Being alert and mindful** of what we are doing must also run through every part of prayer. Our thoughts mustn't be allowed to wander when we come to talk with the holy God, otherwise, we will leave God in the middle of prayer because the temptations from Satan and from our own hearts are strong. Without being alert, our worship will just become a formality, and our hearts will be cold and indifferent. We are reminded, "Therefore be self-controlled and sober-minded for the sake of your prayers" (1 Peter 4:7).

To these, we can also add humility and delight, and other holy emotions, but I will mention them more in the next section.

Grace in the Parts of Prayer

The grace that belongs to these can be distinguished according to the parts of prayer:

1. Calling on God requires a special awe of his majesty to accompany it, and a deep sense of our own humility and unworthiness. At the same time, we should express wonder and pleasure that the most high God, who inhabits eternity, allows wicked and worthless beings like us to communicate with him.
2. Praise lists the many attributes of God's nature and requires us to display suitable emotions for those attributes. When we mention God's self-sufficiency and independence, it is good to be humble and acknowledge our dependence. When we speak of his power and wisdom, we should recognize that we are weak and foolish, and stand in awe at the glory of God. When we mention his love and compassion, our hearts should love him too. When we think of his justice, we should have a reverence and a religious fear to be in the presence of a just God. And the thought of his forgiveness should bring us hope and joy.
3. In confessing our sorrows and sins, humility is a necessary grace, as well as deep contrition of the heart, in the presence of God whose laws we have

broken, the gospel we have abused, majesty we have disregarded, and whose vengeance we deserve. All the springs of repentance should be opened, and we should mourn for sin at the same time that we hope it is forgiven and our souls are reconciled to God. Shame and holy anger against the corruption of our hearts should also be in this part of prayer.

4. In our requests, we should be as passionate about the nature of what we are asking. When we pray for eternal things and blessings, we should be enthusiastic and eager in our desires. When we ask for provisions and needs, the intensity of our zeal should be less, because it is possible to be happy without receiving many of the things we want. Submission is needed here. God expects to see his children wise enough to discern between the things that are according to his will and most necessary for our happiness.

While we make intercession for our friends or enemies, we should feel compassion. And when we pray for the church, we should have a burning zeal for his glory and a love for our fellow Christians.

1. Pleading with God needs humble persistence. The arguments we use with God in pleading with him are different ways of persistent request. But because we are just people, and we speak to God, humility must be in every one of our arguments. Our pleadings should be expressed as carrying that decency and

distance that is expected of us in the presence of our Maker.

In pleading, we are also required to have faith in the promises of the gospel, faith in the name of Jesus our Mediator, and faith in the mercies of God according to his Word. We are called to believe that he rewards everyone who diligently seeks him (Heb. 11:6); that he is a God who hears prayer and will give us what we seek, according to his glory and our salvation.

The grace of hope also comes into exercise here. While we trust the promises, we hope for the things promised or the things we ask for. We must stay humble in our expectation of those mercies for which we plead with God. We must direct our prayer to him and look up with David (Psa. 5:3), and, with Habakkuk be alert and see what he will say to us (Hab. 2:1).

1. In the declaration or dedication, humility is required again: submission to his will, a composed, quiet spirit even if, in his wisdom and love, he does not give us the things we seek. Then we need the patience to work, and remain humble, waiting on God. With a steadfast spirit and courageous heart against all oppositions, we are dedicated to the Lord.
2. In thanksgiving, gratitude of the heart is required: a deep sense of favor and proclaiming God's goodness to the best of our ability; a growing love for God, and sincere longing to do something for him, because of his

grace towards us. With holy wonder, we acknowledge that God gives mercies to us who are so unworthy. This wonder should grow into joy as we bless our Maker for everything he gives us and our Father for his covenant and love. In our thanksgiving, we should take notice of all the times God has answered our requests. It is a poor relationship we have with God if we only care about what we say to him, but take no notice of any replies he makes to our worthless pleas.

3. When we bless God, we should show a desire to honor the name of God, and our hearts should long for those promises to be fulfilled that his glory may be spread and to magnify his own name and the name of his Son. We should rejoice in the glories of our God that he will have forever.

4. Then we conclude the whole prayer with our Amen of sincerity and faith, in one short word expressing again our praise, confessions, and requests, our trust, and hope that our prayers and hearts are acceptable. We should be encouraged to go from prayer calm, composed, and joyful as someone who has been with God.

But if some people become discouraged because they do not find faith, hope, love, passion, and delight in worship, and think that they do not have the grace of prayer, I would add this warning: each grace of prayer is not always noticeably at work in the heart at the same time. Sometimes one is more evident, and sometimes another, in our weak and imperfect state.

And when a Christian comes before God with a dry, dead heart, overcome with carnal thoughts, and feels reluctant to even pray, and falls down before God, mourning, complaining, guilty, and with sighs and deep groans makes their burden and sins known to God; though they cannot say much, their attitude will be approved of by God who judges the secrets of the heart and makes allowances for the weakness of our flesh. He will acknowledge his own grace working in that heart, even though it is struggling through loads of sin and sorrow.

Suggestions to Gain the Grace of Prayer

To direct us to pray spiritually, we must see it as a holy conversation between earth and heaven, between the holy God and sinful beings. These are the logical rules to maintain this type of conversation:

<u>**Suggestion 1:**</u> Let your heart understand who the two parties are that maintain this communication: God and yourself.

This is one suggestion for the gift of prayer, but it is also necessary to attain the grace. Let us consider who this glorious being is who invites us to fellowship with himself: awesome in majesty, fearsome in righteousness, irresistible in power, unsearchable in wisdom, all-sufficient in blessedness, and condescending in mercy. Let us remember who we are, invited to this communication: wicked in nature, guilty in our hearts and lives, needy of every blessing, utterly incapable to help ourselves, and miserable forever if we are without God!

If we have sincerely obeyed the call of the gospel and have some hope of his love, let us consider how we are forever grateful to him, and how delightful it is to enjoy the visits of the One who will be our joy to live with forever. When our spirits are moved with such thoughts, we are in the best attitude and most likely to pray with grace in our hearts.

Suggestion 2: When you come before God, remember the nature of this conversation.

It is all spiritual; remember the dignity and privilege, the purpose and the importance of it. A sense of the favor in being admitted to this privilege and honor will fill our hearts with wonder and joy, that is found in the favorites and worshippers of an infinite God. Attention to the purpose and importance of prayer will fix our thoughts to become more alert; it will cause your spirit to become serious; it will command all your inner strength to devotion, and it will raise your desires to holy passion. You pray to him who has power over your eternal salvation or eternal destruction, to save and to destroy. If eternity will not awaken some of the graces of prayer, the heart must be in a very dull and insensitive state.

Suggestion 3: Seek the friendship with of the One you communicate with and strive for hope and assurance of that friendship.

We are all enemies of God and children of his wrath (Rom. 8:7; Eph. 2:2). If we are not reconciled, we can never communicate with him. How can we enjoy talking with an enemy so almighty or worship him, while we believe he hates and will destroy us? But how unspeakable is the pleasure of holding a conversation with such an infinite, almighty, and compassionate friend? And how ready is nature to give him all the honor, while we feel and know ourselves to be his favorites and the children of his grace; while we believe that all his honor is our glory in this friendship, and each of his perfections is the pillars of our hope and the assurances of our happiness?

In order to obtain this friendship and find this holy fellowship, we need to look at the next suggestion:

Suggestion 4: Live in and with Jesus the Mediator, who is the only one that can bring you near to God.

Jesus is the way, the truth, and the life; no one comes to the Father but by him (John 14:6). Through him, Jews and Gentiles have access to the Father (Eph. 2:18). Live in him by trust and dependence, and live with him by meditation and love.

When a sinner is first convicted and sees the awesome holiness of God and his own guilt and deserved damnation, how afraid he is to draw near to God in prayer, and how discouraged he is without hope! But when he sees Jesus as our mediator and his ability to save; when he first sees this new and living access to God, consecrated by the blood of Christ, how joyfully he comes before the throne of God and pours out his heart in prayer! And how passionate is his nature in every grace of prayer! How deep his humility! How zealous his desires! How persistent his pleadings! How exuberant his thanksgiving!

We always need to keep a deep sense of the evil of sin, our deserved death, the holiness of God, and the impossibility of our communication with him without a mediator, so that the name of Jesus will be precious to us, and so that we may never come into God's presence in prayer without our hearts before Christ, our glorious introducer.

Suggestion 5: Always keep a praying character, an attitude ready to talk with God.

This is the one way to keep all praying graces ready to use. Often and in every occasion, visit him in personal and secret prayer. Make prayer your delight, and do not become satisfied until you find pleasure in it.

Whatever advantages and opportunities you enjoy for public prayer, do not neglect to pray in secret. At least once a day, stop your busy life, to say something to God alone.

When you join with others in prayer and you are not the speaker, let your heart be ready and alert, that you can pray better when you are the mouth of others to God.

In the middle of your work and duties, lift up your heart to God as often as you can. He is ready to hear a sudden sentence, and he will answer the whispers of a heart towards him in the short gaps or spaces between your daily affairs. In this way, you can pray without ceasing, as Paul commands, and your graces will always be active. If you only address God in the morning and evening and forget him during the day, your heart will grow numb; you will worship only with your lips and your knees and fulfill the task out of habit.

Suggestion 6: Seek the help of the Holy Spirit.

He works every grace in us and equips us for every duty; he stirs sleeping graces into action; he draws the heart near to God and teaches us this communication with heaven. He is the Spirit of grace and supplication, which we will look at in detail in the following chapter.

Study Guide

In the context of this chapter, grace describes the characteristics that are ours simply because of Jesus' death and resurrection. Instead of working to achieve them through following the law, and instead of striving to be righteous, we have access to all this in grace. In prayer, we can now have faith, boldness, and many other qualities since Jesus has made a way for us to have them.

1. What is the difference between grace and gift in this chapter?
2. Read Romans 5:15 and 2 Corinthians 9:8. What is your understanding of grace in prayer?
3. How can the gift of prayer be attained? Can grace be attained in the same way?
4. How does grace change the way or manner in which we pray? Look specifically at the parts of prayer in relation to the characteristics we now have through grace.
5. The last suggestion says that we need the Holy Spirit's assistance in gaining grace in prayer. Why is this important?
6. Which one is easier for you when it comes to praying —the gift or the grace? Why?

4

THE SPIRIT OF PRAYER

All the rules and suggestions to teach us to pray will be useless if we have no spiritual assistance. We do not have the ability to think one holy thought, and all that is good comes from God. If we want to attain the gift or grace of prayer, we must seek them both from heaven. And since the gifts of God that are given to men are usually attributed to the Holy Spirit, he can possibly be called the Spirit of prayer. We need to ask for his help diligently and persistently.

The spirit of prayer in our language often describes a state of mind well equipped and ready for prayer. So when we say that there was a greater spirit of prayer found in churches before, we mean that there was a greater degree of the gift and grace of prayer amongst people; their hearts and mouths were better equipped and fitted for it. But to deny the spirit of prayer in all other senses, and declare that there is no need for the Holy Spirit to assist us in praying, borders on blasphemy in our self-sufficiency.

In this chapter, I will first prove by plain and easy arguments that the Spirit of God does assist his people in prayer, and then show how he does this, and to what extent so that we may not expect more from him than the Bible promises nor too little. After a few warnings, I will give some suggestions and advice on how the Holy Spirit's help can be obtained.

Proof of the Spirit's Help in Prayer

1. *From the Bible*
2. *"And I will pour out on the house of David and the inhabitants of Jerusalem a spirit of grace and pleas for mercy"* (Zech. 12:10). The Holy Spirit is called a Spirit of supplication in respect to the operations and outcomes he is promised to fulfill in this verse. His work amongst men is often expressed in being poured out on them (Isaiah 44:3; Prov. 1:23; Titus 3:6, and many other places). Now it is evident that this prophecy refers to the gospel because it is looking to Jesus as being pierced or crucified. *"When they look on me, on him whom they have pierced."*

Objection: Some will say this promise refers only to the Jews at the time of their conversion.

Answer: Most of these great promises that relate to the New Testament are made specifically to Jacob, Israel, Jerusalem, and Zion, in the language of the Old Testament. We would deprive ourselves, and all the Gentile believers, of every one of these promises in an instant through such a narrow view! Paul sometimes quoted promises from the Old Testament made to the Jews and applied them to the Gentiles, as, *"I will make my dwelling among them and walk among them, and I will be their God, and they shall be my people..."* (2 Cor 6:16-18), which is written for the Jews (Lev 26:12). *"...be separate from them, says the Lord, and touch no unclean thing"* is taken from Isaiah 52:11 and Jeremiah 31:1,9, where Israel is mentioned. And yet, in 2 Corinthians 7:1 Paul says, *"Since we have these promises, beloved, let us cleanse ourselves."* And so he makes the Corinthians possessors of these same promises.

He also encourages us to do the same when he tells us, *"Whatever was written in former days was written for our instruction, that through endurance and through the encouragement of the Scriptures we might have hope"* (Rom. 15:4). And he assures us (verses 8-9) that Jesus Christ confirms the promises made to the fathers, that the Gentiles may glorify God for his mercy.

"For all the promises of God find their Yes in him. That is why it is through him that we utter our Amen to God for his glory" (2 Cor. 1:20). Now it would have served little purpose to have told the Romans or the Corinthians of the stability of all the promises of God if their faith might not embrace them.

We are said to be blessed with faithful Abraham if we are imitators of his faith (Gal. 3:29). If we are Christ's, then we are Abraham's seed, and heirs according to the promise; heirs by faith of the same blessings that are promised to Abraham and to his seed (Rom. 4:13). Now this very promise, the promise of the Spirit, is received by us Gentiles as heirs of

Abraham (Gal. 3:14), that the blessing of Abraham might come on the Gentiles through Jesus Christ, that we might receive the promise of the Spirit through faith.

Having an interest, therefore, in his covenant, we have a right to the same promises, as far as they contain grace in them, that may be properly communicated to us. And so, in this prophecy of Zechariah, it not only signifies the natural descendants of David the king, but includes the family of Christ, the true David—believers that are his children, inhabitants of Jerusalem, and members of the church, whether they were originally Jews or Gentiles. For in Christ Jesus men are not known by these distinctions; there is neither Jew nor Greek (Gal. 3:28).

1. In Luke 11:13, after Christ had answered the request of his disciples and taught them how to pray by giving them a pattern of prayer, he recommends that they ask his Father for the Holy Spirit, for a fuller and further assistance and instruction in prayer, as the whole passage seems to mention.
2. *"Likewise the Spirit helps us in our weakness. For we do not know what to pray for as we ought, but the Spirit himself intercedes for us with groanings too deep for words"* (Rom. 8:26). This cannot be interpreted as if the Holy Spirit does Jesus' work, who is our proper intercessor and advocate. The Spirit, not being clothed in human nature, cannot properly be represented under such an inferior character, as the nature of prayer or petition seems to imply, whereas Jesus, being man as well as God, can properly assume the role of a petitioner.

The duty of the Holy Spirit, therefore, is to teach and help us to plead with God in prayer for the things we want. And this is evident in the next verse.

3. "*God has sent the Spirit of his Son into our hearts, crying, 'Abba! Father!'*" (Gal. 4:6). The Spirit teaches us to address God in prayer as our Father. And so it is explained. "*You have received the Spirit of adoption as sons, by whom we cry, 'Abba! Father!'*" (Rom. 8:15). It may be noted here that this Spirit of adoption belongs to every true Christian, otherwise Paul's reasoning would not be strong and convincing. "*Because you are sons, God has sent the Spirit of his Son,*" etc.

4. "*Praying at all times in the Spirit, with all prayer and supplication. To that end, keep alert with all perseverance*" (Eph. 6:18). These words 'enpneumati' (in the Spirit) refer to the work of the Spirit of God in us, just as they signify in other places of the New Testament: "*It is by the Spirit of God that I cast out demons*" (Matt. 12:28); "*He came in the Spirit into the temple*" (Luke 2:27); "'*For to one is given through the Spirit the utterance of wisdom, and to another the utterance of knowledge according to the same Spirit, to another faith by the same Spirit, to another gifts of healing by the one Spirit*" (2 Cor. 12:8-9). In this verse of the letter to the Ephesians, it cannot mean praying with our own spirit, with our own minds, because that is implied in the next words, "*To that end, keep alert with all perseverance, making supplication for all the saints.*"

Objection: Some will still say that this praying in the Spirit was only to be performed by an extraordinary gift given to the apostles and others in the first age of Christianity; something like the gift of tongues at Pentecost, and various gifts among the Corinthians, when they prayed, preached and sang by inspiration (1 Cor. 14).

Answer: Whatever extraordinary and miraculous gifts of the Spirit were given in those first days of the gospel, we are not saying that we have the same now. But the assistance of the Spirit that we speak of is available to Christians in every age in some measure, for in this verse (Eph. 6:18), praying in the Spirit is required of all believers, and at all times, with all sorts of prayer. Now, it is not to be supposed that at all times and in all sorts of prayer Christians should have this extraordinary gift.

We can also add that the gift of prayer itself is not expressed as an extraordinary and miraculous gift in the prophecy of Joel 2, or in Acts 2, where it is fulfilled. Nor is it mentioned among the miraculous gifts of the Holy Spirit in the epistles of Paul. But only the gift of prayer in an unknown tongue is spoken of in 1 Corinthians 14, which refers to the gift of tongues rather than to that of prayer. It is not unlikely that by not mentioning the gift of prayer in those verses is for this very purpose: though there were gifts of prayer by spiritual inspiration in those days, there should be no bar against Christians of some spiritual assistance in prayer, by believing that this was a gift only for the apostles and the first Christians.

1. *"The prayer of a righteous person has great power as it is working"* (James 5:16). In the original, it is translated as 'inwrought' prayer, which described people

possessed with a good or evil spirit. Here it signifies prayer wrought or implanted in us by the good spirit that possesses, leads, and guides us. The word is used in this sense several times in 1 Corinthians 12, where the gifts of the Holy Spirit are mentioned. But notice that here James is speaking of an inwrought prayer that all Christians are capable of, for his letter is directed to all the scattered tribes of Israel (James 1:1). He tells them all to confess their faults to one another and pray for one another, that they might be healed because the inwrought prayer of the righteous has great power in it.

2. *"Praying in the Holy Spirit, keep yourselves in the love of God"* (Jude 20-21). This was written to all that are sanctified by God the Father, preserved and called in Jesus Christ (verse 1). They are all directed to pray with the assistance of the Holy Spirit. Those who do not have this Spirit are said to be sensual (verse 19).

3. There are many supplementary verses that represent the Spirit as the spring of all that is good in us and show us that all other tasks in the Christian life are to be performed in and by this Holy Spirit.

Christians are born of this Spirit (John 3:6); are led by the Spirit (Rom. 8:14); walk in the Spirit (Gal. 5:16); live in the Spirit (Gal. 5:25), and by this Spirit put to death the deeds of the body (Rom. 8:13). The Spirit convinces us of sin (John 16:9) and equips us for confession. The Spirit witnesses with our spirits that we are the children of God (Rom. 8:16) and thereby fills us with thanksgiving. The Spirit sanctifies us and fills us with love, faith, humility, and every characteristic that is needed in prayer. Why then should people make such an effort to block us from praying by the Spirit, when it is only by this Spirit we can walk with God and have access to God (Eph. 2:18)?

The Holy Spirit has been ignored or not been present in the church for so long that we are tempted to think that all his work in encouragement, prayer, and preaching, belongs only to the early Christians and to super-spiritual ministers, prophets, and apostles. Because of this absence, people have invented various methods to compensate for the lack of Spirit in prayer, by paternosters, beads, litanies, responses, etc. They were designed to keep the form of worship and the attention of the people. We have had many teachers that have urged us to use our natural powers, reason, and memory. From all of this, criticisms about the Spirit of prayer, and attempts to make this word mean nothing more than a state of the mind that has arisen. So the Spirit of adoption is nothing but a childlike attitude, and the Spirit of prayer is just a praying state of heart.

But since some verses speak specifically of the Holy Spirit as working these things in us, and the Spirit of God being promised to us, to live and be in us, and to assist in prayer, why should we exclude him from the hearts of Christians and throw him out of those verses that clearly point to the opposite? In my opinion, it is more logical and reasonable to interpret the places in which the Spirit is mentioned according to clear verses where his name is written.

However, if a person wants the Spirit and his help in prayer to be mentioned in any verse to be persuaded and encouraged to seek that assistance that they can pray better, it is not an issue if they cannot find this Spirit in every passage where others believe he is spoken of.

1. *From Christian Testimony*

The major difference between some believers and others in this respect, even where their natural abilities are equal, and the difference in believers themselves at different times, seems to be the presence or absence of the Holy Spirit. Some people in special times will break out into a spiritual prayer and be carried far beyond themselves. Their thoughts, desires, and language all seem to have something of heaven in them.

I am sure that in some people this can be due to their incredible understanding, intelligence, sensitivity, memory, natural thinking, and eloquence. But often, people who have this gift of prayer are not above or on par with other Christians in sensitivity, intelligence, passion, or eloquence. They might possess little skill and are below the average capacity of others. It is not always just an overflow of enthusiasm and imagination, for this often happens when they find their natural spirits are not positive, but discouraged or under pressure, and they can hardly speak or think about normal things. I wish there were more testimonies to the help of the Holy Spirit among us.

<u>Reflection:</u> Those who despise this gift of the Holy Spirit will mock those who claim to share in it as foolish, stupid, ignorant people, and will say they are uneducated, dull, and clueless. And yet when the objection is made, 'Where does

this eloquence come from, this passion, and this ability to pour out the heart before God in prayer, which those who mock cannot even imitate? Then they say it is quick-thinking, good memory, innovation, sensitivity, our passion, confidence, or persistence—anything but the Holy Spirit because they have decided to oppose his power and deny his work in the hearts of believers.

To confirm the belief that the Holy Spirit assists us in our religious performances, I will add citations from the Articles and liturgy of the Church of England: "We have no power to do good works, pleasant and acceptable to God, without the grace of God by Christ preventing us, that we may have a good will, and working with us when we have that good will" (Ant. 10). "The working of the Spirit—drawing up the mind to high and heavenly things" (Ant. 17). And this ordinary work of the Holy Spirit in all believers is called the "inspiration of the Holy Spirit" (Ant. 13).

"God from whom all holy desires, all good counsels, and all just works do proceed;" and a little after; "Almighty God, who has given us the grace to make our common supplications" (Second Collect at Evening Prayer). "Grant that by your inspiration we may think those things that are good, and by your merciful guiding may perform the same" (in the Collect, the Fifth Sunday after Easter). "Almighty God, of whose only gift it comes that your faithful people do to you true and acceptable service" (13th Sunday after Trinity). "Grant that your Holy Spirit may in all things direct and rule our hearts" (19th Sunday after Trinity).

Homily 16th pages 1-2, asserts the "secret and mighty working of God's Holy Spirit which is within us: for it is the Holy Ghost, and no other thing, stirring up good and godly motions in their hearts." Many more expressions of this kind might be collected from the Homilies and public prayers of the Church of England, so no one would think of rebuking and mocking the help of the Holy Spirit in good works and religious duties.

How the Spirit Helps in Prayer

It is evident, then, that there is such a thing as the assistance of the Spirit of God in prayer. Just how far this assistance extends is a further subject of inquiry. And it is necessary to have a proper understanding of the nature and limits of his influence, that we may not expect more than God has promised, nor be unaware of the help that is available to us.

People often go to extremes on such a subject—they attribute either too much or too little to the Holy Spirit.

In my judgment, these people attribute too little to the Spirit of prayer:

1. Those who say that there is no more help expected in prayer than in any ordinary events of life. For example, when a farmer plows the land and throws in seeds, God instructs him and teaches him (Isaiah 28:24-26). But this denies the Spirit's special influences.
2. Those who allow the Spirit to stir their hearts while they pray, and to awaken grace according to the

words of a prayer; but say that he does nothing in gaining the ability or gift of praying, nor assists in using the gift with proper content, method, or expression.

I am sure that the verses from the previous section concerning praying in the Spirit can never be explained this way in their full meaning. I want to make it clear that the Holy Spirit has more to do with prayer than both these opinions allow.

On the other hand, there are people who expect too much from the Spirit:

1. Those who wait for every suggestion to pray as dictated by the Spirit, and will never pray unless he moves them. In Scripture, there are many encouragements and commands to pray on every occasion. But, I find no promise or encouragement to expect the Holy Spirit to dictate to me through feelings and impulses every time of prayer. Even though the Spirit sometimes withdraws his influences, my duty and obligation to pray continuously still remain.
2. Those who expect help from the Holy Spirit to make their prayers inspirational, like the prayers of David, Moses, and others in the Bible. Let us not think that the work of the Holy Spirit in ministers, or in common Christians while they teach, exhort, or pray, are the same as those miraculous gifts that were given to the apostles and early believers, described in

the church of Corinth and elsewhere. For at those times a whole sermon, or a whole prayer together, was a constant impulse of the Holy Spirit, maybe for the words and the content, which made it truly spiritual. But in our own prayers, he often leaves us to ourselves, to mix weaknesses and errors into the content, manner, and words, so that not one sentence is the perfect or the pure work of the Spirit. It would be blasphemy to credit the Spirit with everything that we say in prayer, as well as to exclude his assistance from every prayer of every Christian.

3. Those who hope for the influence of the Spirit so they do not need to study or make an effort. Because they wait for spiritual urges, they've never been diligent in equipping themselves logically to pray. They won't premeditate beforehand but rush into prayer, just like Peter when he jumped out at Jesus' command to walk on the water, and hope to be carried through without their own forethought. They will quote the verse given to the disciples, *"When they deliver you over, do not be anxious how you are to speak or what you are to say, for what you are to say will be given to you in that hour"* (Matt. 10:19).

But this verse means something different. To say Jesus does not allow any premeditation, or anxious and troubled fear and care; just as we are told to not think about tomorrow (Matt. 6:34); not to be over-worried or anxious about provision for tomorrow is wrong. Jesus told the apostles not to prepare as they appeared before the magistrates in specific circumstances. It can never be used to encourage laziness in

Christians in ordinary circumstances when we come before God in prayer.

To find a happy medium between these two extremes, we can look at the Bible. His assistance in prayer can be reduced to the following points:

1. **He enhances our natural abilities** with understanding, judgment, memory, intelligence, and character; some measure of confidence and eloquence; and readiness to speak the thoughts of our mind. He does this for believers as he does for everyone else because every good gift comes from God (James 1:17). The third person of the Trinity, the Holy Spirit, is generally represented as the agent in these kinds of operations, especially when it comes to Christianity.
2. **He blesses our diligence** in reading, hearing, meditation, study, and attempts at prayer. As we find useful rules and instructions to help, we treasure up a store of material and learn to express our thoughts eloquently and decently, for our own and others' edification.

So, as Christians, in order to grow in the knowledge of the things of God, he adds a blessing to our studies: in the learning of tongues to interpret Scripture, and in the skill of exhortation, in order to become able ministers. All these are called spiritual gifts because in the early times they were given suddenly and in a miraculous way, without needing to study to get them. But today these are to be obtained and developed through effort and use, by repeated trials, by time and experience, and the blessing of the Spirit of God.

The same can be said concerning the gift of prayer. He sanctifies our memory, to treasure up verses that can be used in prayer; he helps us to remember them at the right times. If people become skillful in any ability, especially when it comes to Christianity, it is rightfully attributed to God and his Spirit. For if he teaches the farmer to sow and reap wisely (Hab 28:26-29), how much more does he teach Christians to pray?

He gives to everyone the gifts he decides and works them according to his good pleasure (1 Cor. 12:4-11). All other help, when well applied, is made successful by his blessing. We can say to Christians who have the greatest gifts in prayer, *"Who sees anything different in you? What do you have that you did not receive?"* (1 Cor. 4:7). If we do not live by bread alone, but by every word of power and blessing that comes from the mouth of God (Matt. 4:4), then the spiritual improvements of the mind are not gained only through our own works, but by the Spirit who makes our efforts prosperous.

1. **He draws and calls our hearts to pray and keeps them focused.** By nature, we all stray and turn from God, even the best Christian. There is a natural reluctance to pray and engage in spiritual habits. It is only the Spirit that forms a heavenly attitude in us, that makes us ready to always pray, that stimulates us to take time out from our busy lives to go to the mercy seat.

He says, *"Now is the favorable time"* (2 Cor 6:2). The Spirit says to the heart, *"'Seek my face.' My heart says to you, 'Your face, Lord, do I seek'"* (Psalm 27:8). The Spirit says come to God by prayer, as well as to Christ by faith (Rev. 22:17). It is he that gives us the desire towards God and silently hints that we have been heard and accepted. By his motivation, he overcomes our delay and answers the objections of our sinful, lazy hearts. He gives our spirits the freedom to pray and keeps our thoughts from wandering, whether we are distracted by our eyes, ears, imaginations, or suggestions of the devil.

It is the Holy Spirit who keeps us in prayer despite our own discouragement and makes us wrestle and strive with God in prayer, to pour out our hearts before him, and to motivate ourselves to take hold of him, in agreement with the words of the Bible (Gen. 32:24; Rom. 15:30; Psalm 62:8; Isaiah 64:7). The way the Spirit often uses to bring us to prayer and keep us there is by giving us a sense of the necessity and advantage of it or giving us some refreshment or delight in it.

And if the devil draws our hearts away through sudden temptation or sinful thoughts, why is it strange that the Spirit should encourage us back with holy motivation?

1. **He gives us content for prayer through his teaching.** This is the language of the Bible (Rom. 8:26). *"the Spirit helps us in our weakness. For we do not know what to pray for as we ought, but the Spirit himself intercedes for us with groanings too deep for words"*—according to the mind or will of God (verse 27). Every clever explanation of this verse that tries to

exclude the work of the Spirit, and makes it mean something else, is forced and does not stand up well.

It is clear that we do not know what is good for ourselves (Eccles. 6:12), and we often ask for things that will hurt us (James 4:3). We do not really know what we need or the help we actually require. It is the Spirit that convinces us of sin and righteousness—our sin, and the righteousness of Christ (John 16:9-10). He is a Spirit of illumination in everything to do with our faith. He alone searches the deep things of God and knows what God has prepared for believers (1 Cor. 2:9). And therefore, he makes intercession or teaches us to pray for things agreeing with God's will and purpose.

He sometimes also hints at arguments you can use to plead with God, either the name or mediation of Christ or some of his own promises in the gospel because he has promised to reveal the things of Christ to us (John 14:26; 16:13-15). He brings spiritual things to our minds, things that are suited to the parts of prayer. He sets the glory and the majesty of God before our eyes and supplies us with a reason for praise. By reminding us of sin, he equips us for confession; and by causing us to reflect on his blessings, he gives us enough to be thankful for.

If the devil can pluck the good seed of the Word of God out of the heart (Matt. 13:19), then the Spirit can put good thoughts into the heart to prepare and equip us for prayer. These influences are the urging of the Spirit, which Christians of almost every denomination will allow to some degree.

1. **When the Spirit gives us content in prayer, he also influences the method.** Method is the arrangement of the material of a prayer one after another. Since it is impossible to say all of them together at the same time, so it is impossible for our minds to receive all hints from the Spirit at once; they are received successively one after another, as seems good to him.

Sometimes he fills our hearts with such deep regret for our past sins that we break out before God in humble confessions at the beginning of prayer: "Lord, I am wicked; what can I say to you? My iniquities are over my head, there are too many to count." And maybe the heart remains in this state throughout the time of prayer.

Another time he works as the Spirit of joy and thanksgiving, and the first words the mouth says are of gratitude and praise: "I thank you, Father, Lord of heaven and earth, that even though the mysteries of the gospel are hidden from the wise and prudent, yet you have revealed them to babies."

Sometimes the heart is filled with specific desire, or shame because of sin, that almost from every part of prayer, praise, confession, thanksgiving, etc., will find some argument for seeking that mercy and at every turn insert that special request with new arguments and pleadings.

So, even though we make sure the sentences are properly connected, and there is a smooth and easy transition from one part of prayer to another, the order of what we say is under his direction or influence. And if we understand the words of Elihu in a literal sense (Job 37:19), we need help in content, method, and everything when we speak to God, and may even cry out, "Lord, teach us what we should say to you, because we cannot order our speech with our natural logic. We need light and instruction from you to structure our words and put them in order."

1. **The Spirit can also assist in giving proper expression in prayer.** He synchronizes with our natural and acquired knowledge, memory, enthusiasm, eloquence, and confidence that we use to express those thoughts which he has stirred in us. He does this in preaching and talking about the things of God, and especially in prayer, so that we are able to pour out our hearts before God with clear thought and expression so that we are edified as well as those with us. Paul speaks of this boldness to speak as a spiritual gift (1 Cor. 1:5; 2 Cor. 8:7), and he often prayed for this confidence and freedom of speech in preaching (Eph. 6:19; Col. 4:3—4). We can also ask God for it in prayer. It is as necessary for the work of grace in our hearts and the building up of the church, the body of Christ, for which all gifts are given.

I will add that as the Holy Spirit often gives us hints for the content of prayer, he also assists us in expression because that is how we put our thoughts or ideas into proper words. Now, when the heart and body are so united like this, most of the ideas and thoughts of our mind are connected to words that they flow with those ideas or concepts that the Holy Spirit has put inside us. When he has given us some silent hints of what we should pray for, we can hope that he will also enable us to use proper expressions that may convey the same thoughts as those who join with us.

When our minds use verses as the content of prayer, in a way these are words taught by the Holy Spirit, as he promised to remind us of those things which Jesus has taught us. This is very evident when these expressions and the grace of prayer are brought together, which is the next step of the assistance of the Spirit.

1. **He wakes up those characteristics in us that are suited to prayer.** He spiritualizes our natural inclinations, fixes them on proper objects, and increases their activity. When sin is remembered, he awakens anger, shame, and sorrow. When God is revealed in his glory and justice, he consumes the heart with awe and fear. When Jesus and his redemption are on our minds, the Holy Spirit increases our desire and love.

As humans, we are cold and dead to spiritual things; he makes us alive in prayer and keeps us there. He gives us a reverence of God while we praise him. We suddenly delight in God and long for him, with passion and persistence in our requests for spiritual mercies, submission, and surrender to the will of God in temporary things, faith in Jesus, and hope in the promises of the gospel, as we plead with God for an answer to our prayers. He also fills us with joy in God while we remember in prayer his glory and blessings, and awakens gratitude in our hearts.

As these qualities are attributed to the Spirit, so in their constant use they need his further assistance and power, since we are not able to produce one good thought on our own (2 Cor. 3:5), only in God. It is God who works in us both to will and to do (Phil. 2:13). He gives us sincere aims and intentions in our requests; because the character and content of our prayers require the Spirit's assistance. We can see that in Romans 8:26; we do not know what we should pray for, but the Spirit helps us. He influences our minds with the glory of God and our salvation. Otherwise, we would ask for things incorrectly so that we might use them for our own selfish desires.

Even though I have mentioned the Spirit's work in awakening our hearts last, it often begins before the prayer and comes before his other influences or our own efforts in speaking to God.

These general beliefs concerning the influence of the Spirit in prayer show how he equips us for prayer as a habit; encouraging and preparing us for it and assisting us in it. The greatest help in prayer credited to the Spirit of prayer is this: putting our hearts into a praying attitude; motivating us to long for God; hinting at our real needs and of arguments and promises to plead with God; and awakening love, fear, hope, and joy in us for prayer. This is why he is called a Spirit of grace and supplication.

When these increase, the heart will naturally influence the thoughts, memory, language, and voice. Out of the abundance of the heart, the mouth will speak. And for the most part, what we say will be proportional to the amount our hearts are in tune and to the natural abilities of the person praying, except in rare and glorious incidences when people are taken beyond their limits by the presence of the Spirit.

There are people who are not interested in Christianity, only logic and philosophy, and yet have mocked the spiritual help given in prayer. To them, I would ask what is so unreasonable in this doctrine or difficult for a philosopher to believe?

If God has required every person to pray and will hear and reward the humble and sincere worshipper, why is so hard to imagine that he is so compassionate as to help us in what he asks of us? Is he not full of goodness and ready to accept sinners that return to him? Won't the same goodness cause him to assist those that desire and attempt to return? When he sees our spirit is willing but weak, won't he encourage the desires of the heart that already longs after him, and inspire us to pray and worship, and prepare us for his own reward?

The same questions should be asked even stronger to Christians that believe in the Trinity. Do you believe God sent his Son to teach us how to pray? And when we are taught the right way, why won't his own Spirit help us to do so? Has Jesus purchased heaven for us? And won't the Spirit help to ask for that heaven and awaken our desires to seek it?

When the Son of God saw us perishing in guilt and misery, did he come down and save us by dying for us? And when the Spirit of God sees a poor person willing to receive this salvation but is afraid to come into the presence of God, won't he give secret hints of encouragement and help the heart and mouth to ask God who is willing to pardon?

When he sees a humble sinner striving to break through temptations, lay aside worldly thoughts, put fleshly things far away from the mind, and to talk with God alone, won't he give him holy thoughts, stir up a strong devotion, help him overcome his difficulties, and bring him closer to his heavenly Father?

Since he has given him a memory, imagination, and speech, won't he assist when those are directed towards himself, and make them quicker and sharper toward God?

Why is the Spirit mentioned so often in the New Testament as one that helps the salvation of sinners? Why does he have so many roles in the Bible? Why is he so often promised to Christians, to be with them and live in them as an incredible blessing, if he cannot assist people to draw near to their Maker or help the children of God to talk with their Father in heaven? If this is not unworthy for God to do, why should it be unworthy for a Christian to believe and hope for them?

Cautions on the Spirit's Help

Talking about the assistance of the Spirit of prayer, there are many practical cases that arise in the thoughts of honest and righteous people. It is not my purpose to expand on this using these; but in order to prevent or remove some difficulties, I will list these few cautions:

Caution 1: Do not believe that every impulse or sudden instinct of the mind to go and pray always comes from the Spirit.

Sometimes when the conscience is convicted under a sense of guilt and danger, it will force a person to go and pray. It was the same with the sailors on the ship with Jonah, when they were afraid of the storm, they all fell down praying. The Spirit of God in his own way often uses our consciences to carry on his work. But when these impulses to pray are triggered because of some frightening event, or a sudden conviction and worried mind, and they drag us into the presence of God without any help and strength to pray, and without a thought as to whether we will succeed or not, we might find that it was not the Holy Spirit who incited us in the first place. Because he not only assists in prayer, but he also makes us conscious of its success. Sometimes Satan might transform himself into an angel of light just to rush and scare a person to go and pray. But his impulses are often very forceful and badly timed. When we are busy with something that is right for that time, he tyrannically commands us to suddenly and immediately leave everything and go pray.

But the Spirit of God draws us to God at the right time, never pushing aside another necessary task we are doing for God or for others. He is a God of order, and his Spirit always motivates us to the proper duty for that time, whereas Satan would divert us from one task by forcing us away to another, and then leave us in our weakness trying to do it and annoy us with accusations afterward.

Caution 2: Do not expect the influence of the Spirit of prayer to be so intense and clear that you can easily distinguish them with certainty from the urges of your own spirit.

The Spirit often acts towards his people in line with what they have been given, either in a very obvious or in a more unnoticeable way.

In the Old Testament, the Spirit of God often carried the prophets away as though they were lifted into some kind of ecstatic trance. Their style and gesture, as well as the stirring of their hearts, was often different from those of normal people, and it was very clear to themselves, and sometimes to others, that they were under the anointing of the Holy Spirit at that specific time.

In the New Testament, the apostles had a more constant and habitual assistance of the Spirit, even though it was also extraordinary and miraculous. And in a calmer way, they were influenced in prayer and preaching more in line with logical behavior, though without a doubt they knew when they were under the power of the Holy Spirit.

Today, we have no reason to expect extraordinary, miraculous manifestations. The Spirit usually leads us in such a soft and silent manner, in line with the attitude of our own spirits and circumstances of life, that his dealings with us are not easily distinguished from the logic of our own hearts influenced by our own morals. But because of the spiritual tendency and the effects, we know that we had some assistance from the Spirit.

He often works the same way in conversion, sanctification, and consolation. He works so naturally and sweetly with our own spirits that it is not easy to distinguish his working by any passion or strength of influence. His work is best known by the favor and desire for spiritual things that we feel in our hearts, and by the fruits, we bear as a consequence in our lives.

Caution 3: Even though we might not expect miraculous influence or intervention from the Spirit of prayer today as it was in the early church, we should not deny them completely, because nowhere has God limited himself from not doing so.

The main reason that sudden miraculous manifestations that were given are mostly over is that the gospel is now properly established. Yet there have been examples through the ages of extraordinary testimonies of the Spirit revealing the truth of the gospel, both for the conviction of unbelievers and for the instruction, encouragement, and consolation of his own people.

In the conversion of a sinner, the Spirit's work is often gradual, started, and carried on through circumstances, sermons, occasional thoughts, and moral arguments until at last the person has become a new creature and decides to give up themselves to Jesus according to the gospel. Yet, now and then there are some surprising and sudden conversions brought about through the overpowering influence of the Holy Spirit, like the conversion of Paul.

In the consolation of Christians, the Spirit often assists our minds by comparing our hearts with what the Bible says, and makes us see that we are the children of God by revealing the character of adoption in us. This is the way he ordinarily witnesses with our spirits. But there are times when the Spirit of God has spoken consolation in a sudden and direct manner that the poor trembling believer has little choice but to receive it. This has been shown to be a spiritual intervention because of the humility and holiness that has followed.

So it is in prayer. The ordinary assistances of the Spirit given today to ministers and Christians imply no more than what I have described in the previous chapter. But there are times that the Spirit of God has carried a person in worship far beyond their own natural abilities in the use of the gift of prayer, and lifted them up to an incredible level, very close to those spiritual anointings that the early Christians witnessed.

If a pastor in a church service has been enabled to say what he wants to God with such a flow of spiritual eloquence and lay out the cases of the whole congregation before the Lord in such expressive language that almost everyone present can say, "He knew my whole heart." If they have all felt something of a holy power in his words, drawing their hearts closer to the throne and giving them a taste of heaven; if many sinners have been born again and Christians made victorious in grace and received blessings toward glory, I would not be afraid to say, "God is in this place, present with the extraordinary power and influence of his Spirit."

If a Christian has been taught by the Spirit interceding in him to plead with God for some blessing with an unusual amount of humility and heavenly argument that he feels, by some prophetic anointing, an assurance it will be given, and it has; if grace has been evident and tangible in the prayer, and afterward his expectation has been successfully answered, I have to believe that the extraordinary presence of the Spirit of prayer was with him at that time. Dr. Winter in Ireland, several ministers, and other Christians of in Scotland many years ago had visible and glorious anointings of the Holy Spirit's power on them.

If a sincere and humble Christian who has been seeking after the knowledge of some spiritual truth for a long time should suddenly be enlightened while on their knees with a beam of heavenly light shining on that truth with clear evidence and teaching them more in one prayer than they had learned in months of effort and study, I would acknowledge that it was the immediate help and answer of the Spirit of prayer and illumination. Luther was said to have experienced such spiritual moments during the Reformation of the church from Catholicism.

If a Christian who is filled with doubts and fears has been waiting on God, seeking consolation and assurance of the love of God; if while he has been at the throne of grace, he has recognized God as his God, smiling and reconciled, and has seen the work of God in his own heart in a bright and convincing light; and perhaps by some encouraging verse in his thoughts has been assured of his love to God and God's love to him; if that sudden feeling of love has filled him with incredible joy and fired his passion for the honor of his God and Father, I can believe he is sealed as a child of God by the influence of the Spirit of adoption, teaching him to pray and cry, 'Abba, Father.'

But because there have been many arrogant and foolish claims to the Holy Spirit moving in people's hearts, I would make three remarks:

1. These are rare moments, when the Spirit moves in such a sovereign and random manner, according to his own wisdom, that no Christian even expects them—though I am persuaded there are many more moments like these among holy and humble Christians that are never made public.
2. They can be distinguished from the simple effects of a good idea, and the spirit of delusion, not so much by the wonder and intensity of the Spirit's influence, but by how much they line up with the Word of God towards humility and growing holiness. The same rule can be used to judge the rare, as well as the common, assistance of the Spirit.
3. However close our rare and extraordinary moments of anointing come to those experienced by the apostles and early Christians, they fall very short in distinct evidence. For the Spirit of God has not taught us to distinguish any specific parts or passage of an extraordinary prayer, so that people can say, "These are perfect spiritual inspirations." This is because he wants nothing to compete with his written Word as the rule of faith and practice of Christians.

Caution 4: Do not use the gift of prayer as a measure of your judgment concerning the Spirit of prayer.

If we follow this rule, there are three cases in which we may be led into a mistake.

1. The first case is when the gift is enthusiastically used. Be careful of believing that all people who use holy expressions with passion and eloquence are praying by the Spirit; it could be that their behavior and character in the world is sinful and despicable in the sight of God. It is true that the Spirit sometimes gives incredible gifts to people that are not born again. But we must not just believe that everything that is bright and beautiful is the wonderful work of the Spirit unless we have some reason to hope that the person is also a Christian.

We also cannot assume that a noisy gesture, distorted face, strong and loud words are signs of the presence of the Spirit. Sometimes the troubled mind or intense emotions have caused Christians to speak in loud complaints and groanings. David sometimes did this, as we read in his psalms. Jesus himself, when overcome with sorrow heavier than he could handle, gave up strong cries and tears (Heb. 5:7), and we know that the Spirit of prayer was with him. But loud noise and animated expressions can be used as a show of passion and power, covering up the lack of inner devotion. Once, God came to Sinai with thunder and lightning and the sound of a trumpet (Exod. 19). But another time when he visited Elijah, he was not in the earthquake or in the storm, but in the still small voice (1 Kings 19:11-12).

I would not say that the difference between the prayers of one minister and another, one Christian and another, is simply because of the presence or absence of the Holy Spirit. Natural characters, abilities, attitudes, and circumstances can make a great difference. Nor would I credit the difference between the prayers of one specific Christian at different times to the unequal assistance of the Spirit, because many other things may coincide to make them seem colder or more passionate, dull or enthusiastic, in the use of the gift of prayer.

1. Secondly, we could be in danger of making mistakes where there is just a small measure of the gift of prayer. Some people are always ready to say that the Spirit of prayer is absent from the heart of a person who speaks to God if they are not very skilled in prayer; if they repeat the same things over again; if they struggle to find the words or express their thoughts in improper language; if they have no connection between his sentences and there is not much order or method in the various parts of prayer!

Now, people who have hardly any ability or talent should not speak in prayer in a congregation or among strangers until they have practiced in private and have attained more of this holy skill; yet the Spirit of prayer may be very evident in the hearts of some of them. Perhaps they are young Christians only just born again and are beginning to learn to pray. Praying is new to them, even though they are passionate and their hearts alive in grace. And natural shyness can sometimes also block the use of a good gift in prayer.

It could also be that they have very low natural abilities, a poor aptitude, and memory, a lack of words, or difficulty in expressing themselves. These people could be those foolish things of this world that God has called to the knowledge of his Son and filled their hearts with rich grace. But grace does not transform a person's nature from dullness and low abilities into quick thought and vibrant language.

Perhaps they have become unaccustomed to praying in public, and when they are called to it again, they might be much at a loss as to the gift of prayer, even though grace fills their hearts.

Or maybe they are in deep humility and mourning before God under a sense of guilt, or overwhelmed with fears, or battling and wrestling hard with some temptation, or under depression because of sorrow; or maybe as David when he was so troubled that he could not speak (Psa. 77:4).

Or finally, God may keep the use of the gift of prayer from them to punish them with shame and confusion because of something else, and rebuke them for carelessness in seeking after this holy skill of speaking to God, even though some love is still at work in the heart.

Sometimes the Spirit of prayer is given to a humble Christian who uses many thoughtless gestures in prayer or speaks with an inappropriate tone of voice.

Perhaps he was never taught proper manners and etiquette when he was young, and such bad habits are not easily unlearned. We should not despise or be offended at such prayers, but to do our best to separate what is holy and spiritual from the human errors and weakness, and be even more motivated to seek after the gift of prayer for ourselves.

1. Thirdly, we are in danger of making a mistake when the gift is not used at all. Some people have been quick to imagine that they cannot pray by the Spirit except when they use the gift of prayer themselves. But this is a great mistake. Though one person is the mouth for the rest of the people to God, everyone that joins with him can be said to be praying in the Spirit, if all the characteristics that are suited to prayer and its expressions are enthusiastically and passionately engaged. And it is possible that a humble Christian might pray in the Spirit in the secret and silence of their heart, while the person that publicly speaks to God in the name of others has very little or nothing of the Spirit with them, or when the words of the prayer are following a prescribed pattern. Though the Spirit of prayer is never applied to the use of the gift where there is no grace, it is often applied to the use of the grace of prayer without any regard to the gift.

Caution 5: Do not expect the same measure of assistance every time from the Spirit of prayer.

He has not limited himself to always be present with his people in the same degree of influence, though he will never completely leave those whose heart he has come in and made as his temple and residence. Jesus compared him to the wind in John chapter 3. The wind blows where and when it chooses—not always with the same force or power or consistency in blowing in the same areas. The Holy Spirit is a sovereign and free agent who pours out his blessings in whatever measure he pleases and at whatever times he decides.

Those who enjoy lots of assistance from the Spirit of prayer should not presume that they will always experience the same amount or intensity. Those that have lost it to some degree should not despair of never recovering it again. And those who have not yet been blessed with his influence can humbly hope to gain it by seeking and asking.

This naturally leads me to the following section.

Suggestions to Keep the Spirit of Prayer

The last thing I propose is to give some suggestions on how to obtain and to keep the assistance of the Holy Spirit:

Suggestion 1: Sincerely seek after grace and faith in Jesus Christ to be born again.

The Spirit of grace and of supplication lives in believers only. He may visit others since he is the author of some spiritual gifts, but he only lives in Christians—the many temples of the Holy Spirit (1 Cor. 3: 16). He fills their hearts with the sweet incense of prayer ascending up to God who is in heaven. If we are in the flesh, in an unconverted state, we cannot please God, walk in the Spirit, or pray in the Spirit (Rom. 8:8- 9). Only the children of God who receive his Spirit as a Spirit of adoption can do that (Rom. 8:15). Because you are his children, he has sent the Spirit of his Son into your hearts, and it is by faith in Christ Jesus that we receive this Spirit (Gal. 3:14). And wherever he is as the Spirit of grace, he will also be a Spirit of prayer to some degree.

Every Christian that wants to maintain and increase in the gifts of the Holy Spirit must live by the faith of Jesus and depend on him, because the Spirit is given to him without measure and in all fullness, that from his fullness we may receive every gift and every grace (John 3:34; 1:16). As in the natural, so in the spirit, the life and energy that flows to the heart and tongue and all the members of the body come from the head. Jesus who lives in heaven as our intercessor and advocate to present our prayers and requests to the throne will send his Spirit down to earth to assist us in drawing them up. Live in him as your intercessor and your head.

Suggestion 2: Diligently try and acquire this gift or skill, according to the suggestions about content, method, and manner of prayer which have been spoken about already; practice prayer as much as possible, both in secret and with one another, that young habits can grow and be developed.

The Spirit of God will come and bless the efforts of the mind towards acquiring spiritual gifts. Timothy was told to give his attention to reading and meditating on the things of God, and to give himself completely to the work, that his growth in these areas may be evident to all, though he received an anointing (1 Tim. 4:13-15; 2 Tim. 1:6). And we should do the same, even though we are not as anointed as he was.

Though prophecy was a gift the Spirit, in the Old Testament the prophets were often young men who were trained up in the study of spiritual things, that they might be the better prepared to receive the Spirit of prophecy and to use and develop it better. These were called the sons of the prophets (2 Kings 6:1; 2 Chron. 34:22). Paul spent much time and effort in his natural abilities while the Spirit worked mightily in him (Col. 1:29).

Do not think that you are in danger of quenching the Spirit by trying your best to equip yourselves with content or expressions of prayer, because the Spirit of God usually works in and by the use of techniques.

As natural things work, so do the things of grace. We can see this in the proverb: *"The soul of the sluggard craves and gets nothing, while the soul of the diligent is richly supplied"* (Prov. 13:4). We need to use our best efforts and then hope for spiritual assistance because the Spirit of God helps together with us (Rom. 8:26). It is the same when a person takes hold of one end of a burden to lift it and a mighty helper makes his work effective by lifting it at the other end and accomplishing the task.

This was the encouragement that David gave to his son Solomon: *"Arise and work! The Lord be with you!"* (1 Chron. 22:16). While we are motivating ourselves to obey the command of God and seek his face, we can have a solid hope that his Spirit will strengthen us to be obedient and help us in seeking. When God commanded Ezekiel to get up and use his natural strength and abilities to raise himself up, the Spirit entered into him, put him on his feet, and by a spiritual power made him stand (Ezek. 2:1-2).

Suggestion 3: Pray seriously, and pray for the promised Spirit as a Spirit of prayer.

Do not depend on all your natural and acquired abilities, whatever wonderful achievements you experience. Some people have been so disappointed when they have been overconfident when they come to pray to God by the strength of their own intelligence, memory, and self-assurance! What a rush and confusion of thoughts they fall into and become incapable of praying properly! The Holy Spirit will be given to those who ask correctly (Luke 11:13). Plead the promises of Jesus with faith in his name (John 14:16-17). He has promised, in his own name and in his Father's, to send his Holy Spirit.

Suggestion 4: Do not quench the Spirit of prayer by only sticking a set form or pattern.

Even though the Spirit of God might be present and help in grace when we use a set form of prayer, we must be careful of stifling or blocking any good desires and spiritual emotions that are stirred up in our hearts when we pray. If we refuse to express them because we do not want to stray from what is written down before us, we will be at risk of grieving the Holy Spirit and causing him to leave us, because he is the Spirit of grace. In this way, we hinder ourselves from his assistance in the gift of prayer.

While you might borrow the best aids in your time of devotion from those prayers that are written by the Spirit in the Bible, take care not to quench his work by sticking only to those words and expressions. The Holy Spirit can be quenched even by restricting yourselves to his own words. If he had thought that those words of Scripture were sufficient for every desire and need of Christians in prayer, he would have given some hint of it in his Word. He would have required us to always use those prayers, and there would have been no further promise of his assistance in this task. But now he has promised it and has told us not to quench it while we pray without ceasing (1 Thess. 5:17, 19).

Suggestion 5: Do not give in to or get involved in spiritless prayer, in formality and lip service, without a godly attitude and emotion in your heart.

There could be a danger of this formality and coldness in the use of the gift of prayer even when we are not restricted to a form or pattern. How can we think the Spirit of God will come to our assistance if our spirits withdraw and are absent from his work?

Notice the state of your minds in prayer; observe the presence or absence of this assistant, the Holy Spirit. And since we are told to always pray in the Spirit (Eph. 6:18), do not be satisfied with any prayer where you feel no spiritual inspiration towards God through the work of his own Spirit. What a sad character and attitude of those hearts that spend years in prayer and worship, and take part in so many duties and forms of devotion with no Spirit in them.

Suggestion 6: Be thankful for every aid of the Spirit in prayer, and develop it well.

Spread all the sails of your heart to make use of every breeze of this heavenly wind that blows when and where it chooses (John 3:8). Line up with his holy inspirations. Remain in prayer when you feel lifted into a passionate activity because it is the Spirit that makes you alive (John 6:63).

He does not always come in an easily recognizable manner, so be very careful in case you shake him off or close him from your heart, especially if he does not visit often.

Suggestion 7: Beware of pride and arrogance when you feel growth in your spirit, spiritual emotions, and inspiration in prayer.

Do not give yourselves the credit that is due to God in case he is provoked. The gift of prayer in passion and enthusiasm can easily puff up the unsuspecting Christian. But let us remember that God lives with the humble (Isa. 57:15), and to the humble, he gives more grace (James 4:6).

Suggestion 8: Do not grieve the Holy Spirit in your life as you deal with the world.

Walk in the Spirit, and you will not fulfill the lusts of the flesh, nor grieve him so he leaves you (Gal 5:16; Eph. 4:30). Listen and take note of the whispers of the Spirit when he convinces you of sin, and obey his secret hints when he leads to do something, especially prayer, in the right times and seasons. Do not grieve him by your lack of vigilance or by intentional sins; do not resist him, otherwise, he may leave. But rather seek more of his enlightening and sanctifying influence.

If you ignore and reject him while you are in the world, he will not be present in your personal devotions or in the church. If you grieve him before people, he will withdraw from you when you want to come near to God and leave your heart in sorrow and bitterness. Treat him well, with respect, when he comes to convict your conscience or to direct and guide you to difficult and self-denying tasks. Value his presence as a Spirit of knowledge and sanctification, and he will not forsake you as a Spirit of prayer. Live in the Spirit, walk in the Spirit, and then you will also pray in the Spirit.

These are a few short and simple suggestions on how the assistance of the Holy Spirit can be obtained, according to the Bible and the experience of praying Christians. Even though he is a sovereign and free agent, and he mercifully gives us gifts so that we can claim no credit for them, the Spirit of God promises his own presence to those who seek it in the correct way.

I will finish this section with advice to those from whom the Spirit of prayer has withdrawn, left, or disappeared, to help them to find his assistance once again.

1. Be very aware of how great your loss is, mourn over his absence, and cry to the Lord.

Remember the times when you could pour out your whole heart before God in prayer with many rich expressions and passion. Compare those shining moments with the dull and dark times that you now complain of. Go and mourn before God, and say, "How alive I was in all my senses in prayer! How deep was my love! How passionate was my zeal! How overflowing was my repentance, and how joyful my thanksgiving and praises! But now, what a coldness has seized my spirit! How dry and dead is my heart, and how far off from God and heaven I am even as my knees are bowed before him! How long, Lord, how long before you return again?" Beware of being satisfied with rituals and habits without the life, power, and pleasure of Christianity. The Spirit of God will come and revisit the mourners.

When God heard Ephraim crying to himself about his state, he turned his face toward him with compassion (Jer. 31:18-20).

1. Look back and notice what led to the Spirit of God withdrawing himself from you and acknowledge those sins that caused him to leave.

He does not go away and leave Christians, except when they grieve him.

look and see if there is some sin that you have committed, especially one of the body. He hates this, for he is a Spirit of purity. David was right to be afraid after his scandalous sin, that God would take away his Holy Spirit from him (Psalm 51:11).

Recall whether you have not committed a sin of pride against your own light and knowledge. This is a definite way to cause him to withdraw his presence from you.

Ask your conscience if you have not resisted the Spirit when he brought a word of conviction, command, or rebuke to your heart; whether you have not refused to obey some guidance and been ignorant of his hints in any duty or worship. This is enough to cause his resentment and departure.

Reflect whether you have not sinfully neglected personal prayer; rushed through it without spending time there because of your carnal mind and sinful fatigue, or gone through the motions like a boring task because the world called you. It is no surprise then if the Spirit of prayer leaves your prayer room just when the world gives you the freedom to go there. And you can also expect that if you decline your personal prayer, the Spirit will not always be with you in public.

Consider whether you have not grown proud and vain in gifts and growth and provoked the Holy Spirit to leave you alone, to show you your own weakness and insufficiency, and to humiliate your pride.

Cry to him in sincerity, and beg him to reveal the thing that has offended him. And when you have found it, bring it before the Lord. Confess the sin before him with deep humiliation and shame. Hate, renounce, and abandon it forever. Bring it to the cross of Christ for forgiveness, and let it be crucified and put to death. Every day, cry for strength from heaven against it, renew your promise to be the Lord's, and to walk more alert before him.

1. Remember how you first obtained the Spirit of prayer. Read over the suggestions that are listed before, and put them all into practice with a fresh, renewed attitude and spirit.

Was it by faith in Jesus that the Spirit was first received? Then by renewing your faith in Christ, seek his return. He is the one that first gives and restores this glorious gift.

Was it in your effort and diligence that you found the Spirit's assistance? Then motivate your heart to the same diligence in duty, and strive and work to come near the throne of God with every natural ability you have, depending on his secret influence and hoping for his response. If the wind does not blow, pull harder on the oar, and so make your way toward heaven. Do not neglect prayer if you think the Spirit has departed, because without motivating your heart to seek him, you cannot expect him to revisit you.

Was he given to you as an answer to prayer? Then beg God again to restore him. If he does not give you the material for prayer by his special influence, take words from the Bible and say to him, "Take away all iniquity, and return and receive me graciously" (Hos. 14:1—2). Plead with him his own promises that he has made to backsliders who return (Jer. 3:22, Ezek. 36:25) and remind him of the repenting prodigal in his father's embracing arms.

When you have found him, hold him tight, and never let him go (Song of Sol. 3:4). Do not indulge in those foolish things again that provoked his anger and absence in the first place. Receive his presence with thanks and joy. Let him stay with you and maintain all his sovereignty inside of you, and see that you remain in him in submission.

Walk humbly and sin no more, in case something worse happens to you: he could depart again from you and fill your spirit with fear and bondage and leave you with the bitter fruit of your foolishness; he could give leave you for months and years in darkness, and that measure of the gift of prayer you had attained would be so locked up that you will hardly be able to pray at all.

Study Guide

The Holy Spirit is an integral part of prayer and every other part of our Christian lives. It is because of his prompting and gentle assistance that we are able to know how, when, and what to pray for. This is praying in the Spirit. However, it is not always simple—our minds and hearts wander, the Spirit can easily be grieved, and we often fall into praying in our own strength.

As with any study guide, it is always helpful to keep notes, to write down your thoughts, verses that come to mind as you are working through questions, and statements that you are not completely sure of and need further investigation. It's also good to keep a record of your personal journey so that you can see areas that need more attention. Keep your Bible close by, too.

1. Who is the Holy Spirit? What is his role?
2. Many people argue that the Holy Spirit was only for biblical times, not for us now. Do you agree? What is Watts' answer to this?
3. Is there any difference between the way people prayed in the Old Testament and the New Testament? If so, what is it?
4. What different things does the Holy Spirit do for us? A few verses to help you are: John 14:26, John 16:7-

8, 1 Corinthians 2:10-11, 1 Corinthians 12:7-11, Romans 8:10-11.
5. Why is it important to have the Spirit in prayer?
6. Why do you think Watts found it necessary to include some cautions about how the Holy Spirit works in prayer?
7. Have you ever made mistakes in following or listening to the Holy Spirit's guidance as laid out in the cautions? What happened?

5

REASONS FOR LEARNING TO PRAY

There is no need to explain the nature of prayer, to list so many rules and suggestions to teach us this skill, unless we are persuaded of the necessity and usefulness of it. This final chapter will look at some persuasive arguments as to why the skill of praying is worth seeking after.

This part is not aimed at those people who are not sincere in their Christianity and have ridiculed and mocked every kind of prayer including public services and authorized forms. I am also not trying to persuade those who have tasted genuine faith, but because of an irrational and stubborn attachment to liturgies, they have given up any efforts of learning to pray.

Reading through the second chapter on the gift of prayer, those who are still undecided will see that it is not some radical act or empty arguments, but a useful and necessary qualification for all. It is a Christian skill that must be attained in a logical way by using the correct methods and the blessing of the Holy Spirit. If that does not influence those people, then perhaps the instruction and rebuke of an esteemed prominent minister who I have mentioned before can persuade them:

"For anyone to satisfy himself with a form of prayer remains in infancy: It is the duty of every Christian to grow and increase in all the duties of Christianity, gifts as well as graces."

How can a man live according to these rules but not make any attempts or efforts to grow? If it is wrong not to try and work to gain this gift, then it is even worse to make fun of it and despise it by calling it spontaneous prayer, and praying by the Spirit—this is what some people call it, but it just shows their unbelieving heart. They are strangers to the power and support found in prayer.

Instead, I want to speak to those who understand their obligation to prayer and how impossible it is to restrict their needs by a set pattern or form, but because of their spiritual mediocrity and reserved approach to Christianity, they do nothing to acquire the gift. They are content to remain average, or worse, and never get any better. It is this sort of Christian that I want to motivate and wake up to diligence in seeking such a valuable gift and skill.

The qualification I suggest does not consist in excellent opinions, fancy phrases, and fine eloquence, but simply in a supply of spiritual thoughts, which are the best materials of prayer, and an eagerness to express them in plain, clear words with a free, natural decency.

Prayer Is Corresponding With Heaven.

The first reason is based on the purpose and dignity of prayer.

Who does not want to correspond with heaven? Who would not be willing to learn to pray?

This is the language in which God gave to the sons of Adam, who are just worms and dust, to address the king of glory, their Maker. Is there anyone among the sons of Adam that does not want to learn this language? Will worms and dust refuse this honor and privilege?

This is the speech that the children of God use when they talk with their heavenly Father. Shouldn't all the children know how to speak it?

This is the manner and behavior of a Christian, and these are the expressions of their mouth as they stand before God. Shouldn't every person know and use this manner of conversation so that they can join in with all the Christians and have access to God?

There are some sincere Christians who worship and pray to God daily, and yet they are often without content or matter and are at a loss for proper expressions. They only have a low attainment of this skill. But it is not their honor or interest to perform such a holy task with so many human weaknesses, and yet be satisfied with them. They are like children who can only cry after their father and stammer out a broken word or two so that he can understand what they are trying to say. They are babies who have not grown up. The Father would rather see his children maturing to adulthood and daily using that broad and free conversation with himself which he allows and to which he graciously invites them.

Prayer is a sacred and appointed method to gain all the blessings that we want, whether they relate to this life or the life to come. Shouldn't we know how to use the method God has appointed for our own happiness? Will this glorious privilege lie unused because of our own neglect?

If the task of prayer was nothing else but coming and begging God for mercy, it would be every person's duty to know how to make such requests and present them in a way that suits a human being coming to ask God for something. But prayer extends much further than that. When a Christian comes before God, they have much more to say than just begging. They tell God how much they understand his attributes, and the respect and reverence they pay to his majesty, wisdom, power, and mercy. They talk with him about the works of creation and stand in awe of it all. They talk about the grace and mystery of redemption and are filled with admiration and joy. They talk of all the affairs of nature, grace, and glory; they speak of his works of destiny, love, and vengeance, for now, and the world to come. The subjects of their conversation with God are infinite and glorious.

Shall we be content with sighs and groans and a few short wishes, and deprive our hearts of such a rich, holy pleasure, because we do not know how to express ourselves in prayer and how to speak this spiritual language?

How excellent and valuable is this skill of praying, compared with the many inferior arts and accomplishments of human nature that we work so hard every night and day to obtain! What effort and work do people put in for so many years in college and university to acquire the knowledge of a trade and business in life! The greatest kind of business is between us and heaven and is transacted through prayer.

How much more diligence should we put in to seek the knowledge of this heavenly trade than all these other studies and degrees that only have an earthly reward? How many years of our short lives are spent learning Greek, Latin, and French so that we can communicate with other people or understand the writings of the dead? Is the language in which we converse with heaven and the living God not worth equal effort?

How tirelessly do some people spend studying the art of conversation, that they may be accepted in every group and find the favor of men? Shouldn't the same care be given to seeking all the methods of acceptance with God, that we may approve ourselves in his presence? What a high value is put on human speech or the art of persuasion so that we are equipped to debate and maintain a conversation with other people. This art of spiritual speech, which teaches us to speak the inner thoughts of our hearts, and beg and converse with our Creator through the assistance of the Holy Spirit and mediation of our Lord Jesus—is it not worth that much to us?

Let the value of this gift of prayer be a priority and engage our sincere efforts in proportion to its superior qualities. Let us desire to have the best of gifts with all our hearts, and pray for it sincerely (1 Cor. 12:31).

Prayer Is Necessary and Useful for Christians.

The second reason comes from our character and profession as Christians.

Shall we declare and profess that we are followers of Christ, and not know how to speak to the Father?

Are we commanded to pray always on every occasion, to be constant and passionate in it? Are we content to be ignorant and unable to obey this command?

Are we invited and encouraged by hope to draw near to God with all our needs and sorrows? Are we happy to not learn to express those needs and pour out those sorrows before the Lord?

Has a way been made that we can access the throne by the blood and intercession of Jesus? Are we content not knowing how to form a prayer that can go up to heaven and be laid out before the throne by this wonderful intercession?

Has his Holy Spirit been promised to teach us how to pray? As Christians, are we going to be careless or unwilling to receive such spiritual lessons?

No part of the Christian life is required to be used as often as this one. And it is most inappropriate to always be at a loss to perform this task that is required daily. Does a person who cannot read profess to be a student? Does any man that cannot preach claim to be a minister? It is hypocrisy when we claim to be part of Christianity if we are not able, at least in secret, to speak a few meditations or expressions to continue a little in prayer.

So, remember Christian: this is not a gift that belongs only to ministers or to heads of families, who always have the duty of having to pray in public. These people should be learning to be experts in this holy skill so that they can perform their task to God in their congregations and households with courage and clear minds, with honor and decency. But this task extends much further. Every person who is a part of the church of Christ should seek after the ability to help the church with their prayers, or at least join with a few fellow Christians in seeking God their Father.

I am convinced that Christians would ask each other's assistance more often in prayer on special occasions if a good gift of prayer was more commonly sought and more universally obtained. There would be no need in congregations where a minister is suddenly sick to miss out on public worship and prayer if a sincere, devoted Christian with a good ability in prayer could take that part of the service, and a well-composed sermon and some useful verses from the Bible. This would be very acceptable to God who loves the gates of Zion, and his own public worship, more than all the dwellings of Jacob, or worship of private families (Psalm 87:2).

This gift is necessary wherever public prayer happens. But the necessity of it reaches even further than that. No man, woman, or child is capable of seeking God without having to exercise something of the gift of prayer. Those that are not called or destined to be the mouth of others in speaking to God are still called to speak to God every day.

Therefore, it is necessary for every heart to be equipped with a knowledge of the perfections of God so that they are able to praise them. They should be so acquainted with their own needs so that they can express them specifically and clearly before God, at least in the thoughts and language of the mind. They should understand the encouragements to pray so that they are able to plead with God for supply. They should observe and remember blessings so that they can repeat some of them before God with humble thanksgiving.

Praying Is a Joy and Advantage for Our Hearts

A third reason is drawn from the delight and advantage of this gift to our own hearts and the hearts of everyone that joins us in prayer.

Christians, have you never felt your spirits lifted up from a fleshly and selfish state of mind to a devoted, spiritual attitude through passionate, active prayer? Have you not found your hearts filled with devotion and carried up to heaven with abundant pleasure because of the regular, holy prayers to God in worship? And when you have been cold and ignorant to spiritual things, have you not felt that heavy and lifeless attitude leave because you joined in with the enthusiastic and stirring expressions of someone else's prayer? Have you ever found sweet refreshment from the burdens of your mind or trials and hardships, when in a broken language you told them to your minister and he has laid them before God in words that have expressed your whole heart and your sorrows? And you have experienced a sweet peace and calm in your spirit when you have stood up from your knees after praying with no more tears?

Have you ever wanted the same gift for yourselves, that you might be able to come before the throne of grace and pour out your heart in the same way before your God? What a sad inconvenience it is to live in a world like this, where we have to face so many new troubles and temptations every day, and not be able to express them to God in prayer unless they are written down in a book somewhere! And how hard it is to find the right words in the right format that suits all our different needs and sorrows!

Maybe in other times, you have felt the holy inspiration during public services when someone has been praying with spiritual skill and passion, and you received more encouragement in that prayer than from the whole sermon. At that moment, your heart was completely free of sinful temptations and devoted to God. Do you long to be able to pray this way in your own house and your own room? Would it not be a pleasure to be able to pray like this with their families every day, and for Christians to engage one another when they meet to pray to God the Father and to help one another forward in praise?

When the disciples had just witnessed the devotion of Jesus (Luke 11:1), who spoke as man had never spoken, their hearts were inspired by the words. One of them cried out, *"Lord, teach us to pray"* (Luke 11:1).

So we can see that attaining this gift is a useful instrument of sanctification as well as comfort, by the working power of the Holy Spirit.

But on the other hand, maybe your painful experience has sometimes taught you that passion and devotion have died and almost been quenched by the useless repetitions or weak, wandering thoughts of some Christians that lead the prayer? And at another time, a prayer with beautiful order and language has become annoying and unacceptable because of some inappropriate tones and gestures so that you were tired of listening to them and wished they would soon end.

Who would willingly neglect to attain an instrument so sweet and successful in strengthening Christianity in its power and pleasure in their own hearts and the hearts of all those around them?

Prayer Honors God and Christians.

The honor of God and the reputation of Christianity in the world gives us another reason for learning and taking hold of this skill of prayer.

God is dishonored when we do not worship him with the best that we are able to give him. The work of the Lord must not be done negligently. It is for his honor that we are given the best talents for his service and that we use them in the best manner. This reveals to the world the respect and reverence we have for our Maker; this gives him glory in the eyes of those in the world. But if we completely neglect this gift of prayer, and serve him every day with a few spontaneous thoughts with impolite and improper expressions that never cost us anything but the movement of our lips, we will not be exalting and sanctifying his name among other people.

Sinful laziness and mediocrity in Christianity have caused some people to believe that God is not very interested and worried about outward things. And if they can persuade themselves that they are right, they will believe that anything is alright for the substance and form of their sacrifice. They begin to address God as though he were not a God of order—they speak to him in confusion. Because the heart is the main thing in worship and prayer, like some foolish Israelite, they are not concerned about what animal they offer him as a sacrifice, so long as it has a heart.

But the prophet Malachi thunders with holy anger and jealousy against such worshippers: *"You bring what has been taken by violence or is lame or sick, and this you bring as your offering! Shall I accept that from your hand? says the Lord. Cursed be the cheat who has a male in his flock, and vows it, and yet sacrifices to the Lord what is blemished. For I am a great King, says the Lord of hosts, and my name will be feared among the nations"* (Mal. 1: 13-14). He rebukes us with sharp resentment; he tells us to offer it to the person ruling and governing us and asks if he would be pleased with it.

Now our consciences are sufficient to teach us to take care when we come and speak to an earthly governor or ruler, to have our thoughts well ordered and words well-chosen, and to offer these with a loyal heart. Surely our supreme ruler in heaven should expect the same care in ordering our thoughts and choosing our words, at least to answer all the aims of prayer.

The reputation of Christianity in the world depends a lot on the honorable manner in which we handle prayer. There is an inner beauty in worship that is made up of the reverent attitude of those worshiping and the living exercise of holy devotion. But only God who knows the heart sees this. There is also an outward beauty that comes from a decent and acceptable performance of prayer that is noticed by other people who see us and are forced to acknowledge the excellency of Christianity in the way we practice it.

Where worship and prayer are performed through spontaneous inspiration, a natural order of things and acceptable behavior is required especially in the person who leads the time of worship. This is the design of Paul in his advice to the Corinthians, *"But all things should be done decently and in order"* (1 Cor. 14:40). What he is saying is that there should be sensible conduct, and regular and logical management in every part of worship, so that it gives a natural beauty to our human actions and gives a visible glory to our Christian acts. Where this advice is followed, if an uneducated person or an unbeliever comes into the church, they will also fall down and worship God, and agree that God is truly in you (verse 25). But if you are guilty of disorder in your speaking, and break the rules of natural light and logic in speaking your inspirations, the uneducated and the unbelievers will say you are mad, even though your words may come from the Holy Spirit.

This applies even more to our daily and ordinary prayer times. When an unskilled person speaks in prayer with heaviness and lack of thought, with cheap, incorrect language, with a false and offensive tone of voice, or when they have awkward gestures to the words, it can make it look like a mockery! A whole group of Christians is ridiculed, and the disbeliever says we are mad.

But when a minister or head of a family, with a fluency of their thoughts and language, offers his requests and praises to God before everyone else and observes all the rules of logical decency in his voice and gesture, how much credit is given to our faith, even in the opinion of those who do not agree or like the way we worship! And how effectively does a performance like this refute the necessity of having to follow written formats! It is victorious against the mockery of our opponents, and brings a conviction to their mind that there is something holy and spiritual among us!

I cannot represent this better than in *The Complete Works of George Savile, the first Marquess of Halifax*. An ingenious author and a courtier during the royal reigns of the two brothers, Charles II and James II. He was definitely a supporter of this cause. In the book, he gives his own thoughts about such matters.

He tells us that he does not want the irrelevant wanderings of those who pour out long prayers to the congregation—a barren soil, which produces weeds instead of flowers. By this, they expose Christianity itself, rather than promote people's devotions. On the other hand, there may be too much restraint put on those people whom God and nature have set apart by blessing them with talents and good sense, but also a powerful voice, which enables them to gush out on the attentive congregation with a mighty stream of holy eloquence. When someone is so qualified, educated, and respectable, and they break out into a wonderful, well-delivered prayer, it has the appearance of a holy anointing. They raise and lead the hearts of the congregation in a far better way than the most composed or best-studied format of written words can ever do.

He carries on to say that the people who pray and serve up all their sermons all decorated on the outside, look like statues or men of straw in the pulpit in comparison. But those that speak with such a powerful passion will make others tempted to believe that heaven itself has dictated their words to them.

Prayer Is Simple With the Holy Spirit's Help

A fifth persuasive reason to seek the gift of prayer comes from the simplicity of attaining it with the assistance of the Holy Spirit. I call it easy and simple in comparison to the long struggle and difficulty that people go through in order to acquire knowledge in arts, sciences, or trades in this world. But even so, you cannot expect that there is no pain and effort required.

Some young people may be so unwise as to make two or three bold attempts to pray in public before they have properly learned to pray in secret. And when they are suddenly at a loss and confused in their thoughts, they have given up any hope and told themselves it is impossible. And as they have tempted God by irresponsibly trying to pray without any proper care and preparation, so they have also blamed their own laziness on God, saying it is a gift that God has not given them.

This is the same as if a pupil who had only just begun to read logic should immediately try to publicly debate the topic in school before the other pupils. When they become confused, they suddenly throw the book away, give up their studies and say, I will never learn it, it is impossible. When we try to attain or achieve anything, we must begin regularly and go on gradually toward perfection with patience and effort. If the rules that were discussed in the second chapter for acquiring the gift of prayer are followed, I do not doubt that an ordinary Christian can gain enough of this skill over time that they can fulfill its demands.

Rather than give up and be completely without this gift of prayer, I would try an experiment like this: Once a month, I would write out a new prayer for myself, for the morning and the evening, and for the Lord's Day, according to all parts of prayer described in the first chapter, or out of the verses that Mr. Henry has collected in his book, *Method for Prayer*, one that I recommend to all Christians. I would constantly use it for that whole month, but not confining myself every time to those same words, but being free to put in or leave out, or expand according to what is going on in my heart or the circumstances around me. In this way, as I go on, I would write less and less, until only a few lines or hints of thought or expression, just as ministers learn to slowly move away from their sermon notes in preaching.

After a year or two of this practice, I would become equipped with some kind of ability to pray without the help of notes, always asking God to pour more of his Spirit on me and teach me the skill of praying. Using this method of making short notes for children according to their age, they can be taught to pray while they are still very young.

Objection: A Christian that loves his comfort and time can try to abuse this proposal and say, "If I can use this prayer of my own format and writing for a month, then why can I not use it all my life and in that way, have no more trouble about learning to pray?"

Answer 1: These people need to read the second chapter again, where you can see the difficulties that arise from the constant use of forms and of the danger of being confined to them.

Answer 2: The matter of prayer is almost infinite. It extends to everything we can communicate with our Maker, and it is impossible in a few pages to mention one-tenth of the subjects of our conversation with God. But in writing out new prayers every month, soon we may go through many of those subjects and grow to be habitually equipped for talking with him on all occasions whatever the subject is. This can never be done by sticking with only one or two written formats. Children learning at school to read take out new lessons daily, so that in the end, they can be able to read everything; they would not attain this if they always stayed on the same lesson.

Answer 3: There is a wonderful variety of expressions in the Bible to represent our needs, sorrows, and dangers, as well as the glory, power, and grace of God, his promises and covenant, our hopes and discouragements. Sometimes one expression will suit our thoughts and attitudes at that moment, and at other times, another expression. It is good to have as a large of a supply of this as we possibly can, so that we might never be at a loss to express the inner emotions of our hearts and put those desires and wishes into words that suit them best.

Answer 4: Though God is not concerned with the variety of words and arguments in prayer, because his ways are not like ours, our own minds and beings are affected with such a variety. Our characteristics are drawn into more enthusiastic activity; by our persistence, in pleading with God with many arguments we put ourselves directly under the promise that is made to those who persistently make requests, and we are more equipped to receive the blessings that we seek.

I would make this one concession: If we have the scheme and substance of several prayers already written and suitable for all the most usual cases and concerns of life and Christianity, and if one or other of these is used with sincerity every day—adding new expressions whenever the heart is prompted by God or when new content arises because of some circumstance—this is much better than neglecting prayer altogether or just sticking to one or two formats. And it will be more edifying to those who join with us than a constant confusion of thoughts and annoying attempts if we try to be spontaneous.

But I say this only for those people who are weaker in their gifts and talents, or when the natural spirits are low or the mind just cannot concentrate on prayer. And in these cases, this way of addressing God, which is called mixed prayer, will not end up restricting the sincere, devoted heart to a dead form of worship. It will sometimes prove to be a wonderful growth and release the spirit from its darkness and confinement. It will give it spiritual content and awaken it to a longer and more enthusiastic conversation with God in its own language. To use a plain comparison, it will be like pouring a little water into a pump, where a much greater quantity will be raised from the spring when it lies low in the earth.

Objection: A Christian might decide not to use any compositions or written prayers because they see them as completely unlawful and quenching the Spirit.

Answer: I would humbly reply that there is no danger of that as long as we do not rely on them as our intended end, but only use them as a method to help us to pray, and never confine ourselves to them without the freedom to alter and adapt. A great person once said, "Though set forms made by others are a crutch or help for our insufficiency, those which we compose ourselves are a fruit of our sufficiency. And a man should not be so confined by any premeditated form as to neglect any special infusion, he should prepare himself as if he expected no assistance, and he should depend upon divine assistance as if he had made no preparation."

For younger students, I would add this: If in your private years of study you followed these recommendations and tried this method once a week as I have described, I am convinced that your gifts will be richly developed; your ministerial efforts would be more acceptable to the world; your talents would attract multitudes to your place of worship; the congregation would be lifted in their spirits while the preacher prays with a regular and divine eloquence, and those sermons that are given with such a prayer would be received with double influence and success.

There Are Consequences for Not Praying

The last reason is to convince Christians how necessary seeking this gift is by showing the consequences of neglecting it. If you make no effort to learn to pray, you will fall into one of these three evils:

1. You will drag on heavily in prayer all your days, even in your private rooms and with your family, and there will be so many mistakes and imperfections that it will rob your own heart of a great benefit and joy of this wonderful task and give no pleasure or profit to those who hear you. The ignorant part of your household will sleep under you, while the more knowledgeable will be in pain for you. And perhaps you will sometimes think of correcting the dullness of your prayer by making it longer. But this is to add one error to another and lay more burdens on those who are tired and exhausted.
2. If you find that you cannot carry on in an adequate constant prayer, you will end up performing a morning and evening ritual and be stuck like that from year to year. Even though it might be possible for some people to use a form of written prayer without deadness and formality, those who do not even try to learn to pray because they are lazy, are most likely to fall into the formality and laziness of

using forms, and the power of Christianity and faith is lost.
3. If you have been brought up to hate all types and formats of prayer, but do not know how to pray without them, you will first become inconsistent in prayer, with every little distraction or blockage diverting you away. In the end, perhaps you will stop altogether, and your house and your private room will be without prayer.

Christians, which of these three evils will you choose? Can you be satisfied to slog through life with all these mistakes and cause prayer to become a hatred and a mockery? Or will your minds be satisfied to be restricted forever to a form or two of lazy devotion? Or will prayer disappear from your houses and all appearance of Christianity disappear from you?

Parents, which of these evils do you choose for your children? You tell them to pray every day, you warn them about the danger of being restricted to prayer books, and yet you hardly ever give them any regular instructions on how to pray properly. How can you expect them to live honorable Christian lives in their families and avoid the things you do not allow? But whatever bad consequences they will have to suffer afterward because of this, think about the guilt that will lie at the door of those who never made any effort to show them how to pray.

While I am doing my best to persuade Christians to seek the gift of prayer, surely no one will be so weak as to imagine that the grace and Spirit of prayer can be neglected. Without some degree of influence from the Holy Spirit, the gift cannot be attained. And without the activity of grace, the prayer will never reach heaven or succeed with God. He is not captivated or distracted by the brightest forms of worship if the heart is not there. The thoughts might be very spiritual, the expressions so beautiful and delivered with every sweet and moving accent of speech, but to him, it is nothing more than a beautiful carcass without a heart. It is a simple picture of prayer, a dead picture which cannot charm, a lifeless offering which the living God will never accept, nor will our great High Priest ever present it to the Father.

There is much more that can be said, which is not the purpose of this book. I recommend my readers to those other books that emphasize the necessity of spiritual worship and describe the glory of inner devotion above the best outward performances. Then you will learn the perfection of beauty in prayer, when the gift and grace of prayer are joined perfectly in the secret pleasure and success of it, and filled with attractive power and beauty for others to see. Then Christianity will be displayed as it truly should— holy and spiritual, and shine in all the glory that is capable of doing here on earth.

Study Guide

True to Isaac Watts' style, he covers all the bases by finishing off by explaining why we need to learn to pray. It's clear that even if we can express ourselves well, there is much to learn about how to enter God's presence and what is expected of us if we want to reach his throne. For those who have not given it their full attention, as well as those of us who diligently pray, this is a reminder of why we pray.

If you have been following through the study guide, making notes, and discussing questions with others, now will be a good time to reflect on all you have learned from the beginning of the book until this moment. Hopefully, you will have gained a new understanding, been encouraged, seen growth in certain areas, and been inspired to pray more.

1. Do you find prayer to be a pleasure or a routine process?
2. Do you agree with the statement, "No part of the Christian life is required to be used as often as this one"?
3. What advantages are there in praying to God?
4. How does prayer honor other Christians? Read Colossians 1:27 and compare your answer.
5. Do you agree with Watts' statement that with the Holy Spirit prayer can be simple?
6. Have you ever experienced any of these consequences in your life at times when you may have neglected prayer?
7. Has any aspect of your personal prayer changed since reading this book?

The author encourages us to search further, learn more, and become excellent in prayer. There are many good books that can add to what this book says and even delve into areas that were not covered in this guide. Here are a few classics that were written by faithful Christians that we recommend:

- *A Call to Prayer* - J.C. Ryle
- *The Power of Prayer* - Charles Spurgeon
- *How to Pray Effectively* - R.A. Torrey
- *The Hidden Life of Prayer* - David McIntyre
- *The Still Hour* - Austin Phelps
- *Power Through Prayer* - E.M. Bounds
- *How to Pray in the Spirit* - John Bunyan

ABOUT ISAAC WATTS

Isaac Watts was born in Southampton, England on 17 July 1674. His father was a schoolmaster and a committed Protestant—jailed twice for his public stand on the matter.

Having received a classic education at King Edward VI School, which centered on Greek, Hebrew, and Latin, Watts excelled, showing great promise. At the age of seven, he was writing respectable verses and attracted the attention of a doctor in the town who wanted to sponsor his education further. As a result, he was offered entry to one of the universities where he would be ordained as a minister according to the ruling church of the day. He refused due to his religious affiliation and instead, finished his schooling at a Nonconformist Academy at Stoke Newington.

Accepting a post as pastor at Mark Lane Congregational Chapel in 1702, he became known as an inspiring preacher. He also helped train other preachers and soon found an enjoyment and passion for education rather than delivering sermons himself. As a result, he became a private tutor to a family and subsequently became friendly with the neighbors, the Abneys.

Struggling with health issues, Watts eventually moved into the house in Abney Park where he ended up living for the next 36 years of his life until he died. The vast grounds were laid out by Lady Mary Abney with the help of her tenant, which included walkways featuring Elm trees that led to Hackney Brook where an island of herons was situated.

Watts often visited this spot on the estate, where he found inspiration for many of the books and hymns that he has become renowned for writing. A statue was later erected on the grounds in his honor after his death.

Despite his obvious gift for writing and composing, Watts also broke new ground in the area of how worship songs were written. At the age of 15, when he complained that the singing in the church had no passion, his father challenged him to write better songs.

Rather than be restricted to strictly putting the Psalms to music as the practice had been, he proposed that the words be adapted to include a more New Testament Christian view. This brought new life to worship in the churches with fresh hymns that could be easily understood.

He wrote his first hymn at the age of twenty and went on to produce around 750 more. Many of them were written to be sung specifically at the end of his sermons to emphasize and help the congregants remember what he had been sharing. As a result, he was known as 'Godfather of English Hymnody' with some of the most famous hymns like *When I Survey the Wondrous Cross* and *Joy to the World* are still sung to this day in congregations, festivals, and other gatherings.

He was also a prolific writer, publishing many writings, poems, and books in his lifetime. Among these was a textbook on logic that covered ideas of perception, judgment, reasoning, and method. It was printed in twenty editions and later became the assigned reader in teaching the subject at Oxford, Cambridge, Harvard, and Yale. He followed this with a supplement called *The Improvement of the Mind* in 1741. His many other books centered on Christianity, teaching different aspects and laying down conclusive arguments in its favor.

Isaac Watts was known to be an educated man who was devoted and gentle and had a large heart, which led him to be compared with Philip Melanchthon, the famous German reformer who worked with Luther. As a theologian and philosopher, Watts became known for his ideas, thought, and debates.

Isaac Watts died at Abney Park in 1748 never having married but leaving behind a rich legacy of thought, worship, and faith that can be best summed up in his own words, "I am the Lord's, and he forever mine."

BIBLIOGRAPHY

Crossway. (2001). *English Standard Version Bible*. Crossway Bibles.
Watts, Isaac. (1789). *A Guide to Prayer*.

www.ingramcontent.com/pod-product-compliance
Lightning Source LLC
LaVergne TN
LVHW021236080526
838199LV00088B/4542